Also by David Kamp with Steven Daly

*The Rock Snob*s Dictionary*

THE FILM SNOB*S DICTIONARY

AN ESSENTIAL LEXICON OF FILMOLOGICAL KNOWLEDGE

*Film Snob *n:* reference term for
the sort of movie obsessive for whom
the actual enjoyment of motion pictures is
but a side dish to the accumulation of
arcane knowledge about them

David Kamp with Lawrence Levi

Illustrated by Ross MacDonald

BROADWAY BOOKS   NEW YORK

Portions of the material published herein previously appeared in
Vanity Fair and *GQ.*

PRINTED IN THE UNITED STATES OF AMERICA

BROADWAY BOOKS and its logo, a letter B bisected on the diagonal,
are trademarks of Random House, Inc.

Visit our Web site at www.broadwaybooks.com

Book design by Ellen Cipriano

Library of Congress Cataloging-in-Publication Data
Kamp, David.
The film snob*s dictionary: an essential lexicon of filmological knowledge /
David Kamp with Lawrence Levi; illustrated by Ross MacDonald.
p.   cm.
On t.p. "snob's" appears with a star in place of an apostrophe.
1. Motion pictures—Dictionaries.   2. Motion pictures—Miscellanea.
I. Levi, Lawrence.   II. Title.
PN1993.45.K25 2005
791.43—dc22
2005047245

ISBN 0-7679-1876-2

1   3   5   7   9   10   8   6   4   2

First Edition

Contents

Acknowledgments

The authors wish to thank Aimee Bell; Meghan Dailey; Graydon Carter; Dana Brown; Matt Tyrnauer; Bruce Handy; Steven Daly; Charles Conrad; Beth Haymaker; Alison Presley; Gerry Howard; Suzanne Gluck; Erin Malone; Adam Leff; Ted Kamp; Mike Maggiore; Gabriele Caroti; Josh Siegel; the late Art Cooper; and everyone who has ever shouted "*Focus!*" in a revival house.

An Introductory Note
by the Authors

The Film Snob's stance is one of proprietary knowing-ness—the pleasure he takes in movies derives not only from the sensory experience of watching them, but also from knowing more about them than you do, and from zealously guarding this knowledge from the cheesy, Julia Roberts–loving masses, who have no right whatsoever to be fluent in the works of Samuel (*White Dog*) Fuller and Andrei (the original *Solaris*) Tarkovsky. The Film Snob fairly revels, in fact, in the notion that The Public Is Stupid and Ineducable, which is what sets him apart from the more benevolent film buff, the effervescent, Scorsese-style enthusiast who delights in introducing novitiates to *The Bicycle Thief* and Powell-Pressburger movies.

The Film Snob*s Dictionary seeks to redress the knowl-edge gap between Snobs and non-Snobs, so that normal, nonsociopathic, movie-loving people may A) become privy to some of the good stuff that Film Snobs zealously hoard for themselves; and B) avoid or approach cau-tiously the vast quantities of iffy or downright crappy material that Snobs embrace in the name of Snobbery.

This second service is especially valuable, because the Film Snob's taste is willfully perverse, glorifying drecky Hong Kong martial-arts flicks and such misunderstood works of genius as Mike Judge's *Office Space* and Michael Mann's *Heat* for *no rational reason whatsoever*. The authors of this book, in compiling its entries, have sought to strike the right balance between intellectual curiosity and Snob madness, so that the reader will feel less intimidated about renting a genuinely entertaining film such as Fritz Lang's *M* just because it is "German Expressionist," but liberated from the burden of ever having to watch a Peter Greenaway film.

Who Is the Film Snob?

The archetypal Film Snob is familiar to anyone who has walked through the doors of an independent video store and encountered a surly clerk—hostile of mien, short on patience, apt to chastise you for not intuiting that Wes Anderson's *Bottle Rocket* is in the James L. Brooks section "because Brooks was the movie's executive producer!" Perhaps this clerk has a shelfful of his own recommendations on display—David Cronenberg's *Scanners*, the complete filmography of Steve Zahn, the Italian women-in-prison pic *Women of Devil's Island*, and, oh, *The Human Tornado*, the second of the raunchy Dolemite features that starred the blaxploitation comic Rudy Ray Moore in the 1970s. As you walk up to the counter with your copy of Ron Howard's *A Beautiful Mind*, this clerk heaves an audible, exasperated sigh, dutifully but contemptuously processing the transaction and sending you on your way with your wretched cinematic piffle.

Before videotape players and pay-cable movie channels, the ranks of such Snobs were thin. Film buffs enlisted in campus film societies or went to repertory cinemas for their old-movie and foreign-film fixes, or simply watched whatever faded offerings were indifferently shoved on television via the *Late Show*, the *Million Dollar Movie*, or some other grim rubric. Diehard cineasts who wished to watch one film over and over again really had to work at it, attending the same theater for several consecutive days, or gaining access to a projector by joining their school's AV club (and thereby consigning themselves to leper status socially). But the rise of VCRs and such services as HBO and Cinemax in the late 1970s and early '80s effected a huge change, enabling multiple viewings and wholesale absorption of a film's content and technique. Youngsters who sat impatiently through HBO's airings of Peter Bogdanovich's wilderness-period film *Saint Jack* (1979) because the cable guide promised "nudity" and "adult situations" soon found themselves contemplating Bogdanovich's camera angles, Ben Gazzara's line readings, and cinematographer Robby Müller's lighting. Lo, Film Snobs were being born.

Bogdanovich himself was a transitional figure, an old-school movie buff of the repeat-attendance variety, who, once he managed to insinuate himself into Hollywood in the 1960s, packed his films with knowing echoes of the movies he'd taken in as a youth, parroting Howard Hawks in this picture, John Ford in that. But he didn't come close to being the kind of out-and-out freak that emerged with the eighties' boom in video stores and studio rereleases of their back catalogues. Suddenly, nearly all of film history was laid out for youngsters to pick over, scan, rewind, and dissect, often with the help of Snob-fomenting reissue companies like Criterion, which specialized in laser-disc (and later DVD) "director's cuts" of such films as *Blade Runner* that were abrim with such bonus features as directorial commentary, excised footage, production stills, trivia quizzes, and so on. Video stores themselves emerged as alternatives to film schools, their staffs swelled with dweebs who watched and deconstructed movies all day, occasionally making time to help out customers.

One such video store, Video Archives in Manhattan Beach, California, employed an excitable movie fanatic named Quentin Tarantino. From 1985 to 1987, the young Tarantino evangelized to his skeptical customers on behalf of such movies as the seventies girl-gang picture *Switchblade Sisters* (taking pains to distinguish its genre from the women-in-prison genre exemplified by Jonathan Demme's *Caged Heat*), and engaged in furious arguments with his coworkers on the merits of Shaw Brothers kung-fu pix and the shooty-booty oeuvre of the statuesque Pam Grier. Within a few years, Tarantino was the internationally known auteur behind *Reservoir Dogs* and *Pulp Fiction*—a huge validation for the growing Snob community, since Tarantino's success proved that Snobs knew better than Armani-suited studio schmucks and aged Sydney Pollack types how to make vital cinema, and that it was okay to flaunt one's Snob credentials by relentlessly referencing other movies and earlier cinematic conventions in one's own pictures. Tarantino's triumph also brought to light a crucial difference between the Film Snob and his marginally more presentable cousin, the Rock Snob: The Rock Snob seldom becomes a rock star—he may be thoroughly versed in the ins and outs of what's cool about Iggy Pop and the New York Dolls, but he lacks the idiot-savant charisma and communicativeness of the lithe halfwits who actually perform rock music. Film, by contrast, is a director's medium, naturally hospitable to behind-the-scenes brainiacs with poor dress sense; it's not a huge step from being a maladjusted Douglas Sirk obsessive to being an Academy Award nominee. (For more information on Rock Snobs, see *The Rock Snob*s Dictionary*, by David Kamp with Steven Daly, Broadway Books, 2005.)

The 1990s and 2000s have witnessed an unprecedented flourishing of Film Snobbery, with extra features now a given on any DVD release—enabling you to watch the French- and Spanish-dubbed versions of Sam Raimi's *Spider-Man 2* if you wish, along with the requisite outtakes, making-of documentary, and an "Ockumentary" about the Doc Ock character's graduation from comic books to the screen—and a surge in the ranks of Film Snobs turned filmmakers. The authors of this book have tried to keep pace with cutting-edge developments, but, given deadline constraints, are bound to have missed out on some nascent Snob trends (Sri Lankan snuff films? A new vogue for Mark Hamill's non–*Star Wars* work?). We promise to be vigilant in keeping tabs for the sake of future editions.

B-B-But . . . Why Aren't Federico Fellini and Ingmar Bergman in This Book?

Readers knowledgeable about film will notice the conspicuous absence from *The Film Snob**s Dictionary, apart from passing references, of such titans of foreign cinema as Federico Fellini (*8½*), Ingmar Bergman (*The Seventh Seal*), Akira Kurosawa (*The Seven Samurai*), and Satyajit Ray (the "Apu" trilogy). The Film Snob may indeed know a fair amount about these filmmakers (Fellini in particular, given that his movies' soundtracks were often composed by Snob cause célèbre Nino Rota), but he generally scoffs at them, deeming them to be mere name-drops for bourgeois losers wishing to seem cultured. Watching a Bergman film is so PBS tote-bag, so Mom-and-Dad-on-a-date-in-college, so baguettes-and-Chardonnay. The Snob prides himself on his populist, un-arty taste, favoring, for example, the soapy, over-emotive schlock of India's Bombay-based "Bollywood" film industry over the artful, nuanced films of the Calcutta-born Ray, and the Spaghetti Westerns of the Sergios Leone and Corbucci over anything Fellini ever made. It's a Reverse Snobbery more powerful than the Snobbery it's rebelling against.

Nevertheless, there are certain areas of the received film-study canon that the Snob deems worthy of his attention, if only because they bear an obvious influence on his pet predilections. Without the insouciant sexuality and casual criminality of the French New Wave films, for example, there would have been no *Bonnie and Clyde* by Arthur Penn in 1967, and therefore no lasting American vogue for nihilistic road pictures and shoot-'em-ups, and therefore no 1990s scuzz-cinema capers starring Tim Roth, Patricia Arquette, Vincent Gallo, Juliette Lewis, et al. Likewise, the cinematographer Sven Nykvist's work for Bergman may not cause the Snob any particular excitement, but this same Snob might declare, in his vernacular, that the Svenster's camera setups for Phil Kaufman and Bob Rafelson *kicked ass!* And so, nestled among the entries addressing such Snob lodestars as chop-socky and *Film Threat* are entries on Eric Rohmer and German Expressionism. What the Snob lacks in manners, he makes up for in eclecticism.

Helpful Hints

Given the complexities and interconnections of the Snob universe, cross-references between entries are common and are spelled out in CAPITAL LETTERS for easy identification. The editors have also seen fit to identify certain entries with the Film Snob Vanguard icon ⊕, the presence of which indicates an entity that is held in especially sacred regard by Film Snobs—for example, the French film periodical *Cahiers du Cinéma*, or the tiny but widely feared and imitated *New Yorker* critic Pauline Kael.

Finally, let us express our hope that this book serves to remove the barriers that separate the Snob and non-Snob populations. Life is too short for resentments to fester over this person's lack of knowledge of the Iranian New Wave or that person's braggadocio over his Mexican-wrestling-picture expertise. And *everyone*, it can be agreed, likes *The Wizard of Oz*. Well, except for those who can only tolerate MGM's visually superior but out-of-print *Ultimate Oz* laser-disc edition.

Oh, and the only Tom Cruise movie it's okay for Snobs to like is Ridley Scott's *Legend* (1985).

—*David Kamp and Lawrence Levi*

THE FILM SNOB*S
DICTIONARY

The Film Snob's Dictionary

A  symbol indicates a
Snob Vanguard item, denoting a person or
entity held in particular esteem by Film Snobs.

Agee, James. Fast-living, Southern-born journalist-novelist-poet (1909–55) whose 1940s film criticism for *Time* and *The Nation*—posthumously compiled in the books *Agee on Film* and *Agee on Film, Volume II*—is better known to Snobs than his Depression-era masterwork, *Let Us Now Praise Famous Men*, or his Pulitzer-winning novel, *A Death in the Family*. Presciently recognizing movies as something more than disposable diversion for moony housewives, Agee was among the first writers to take the film beat seriously, glorying in the works of the silent-comedy masters at a time when they couldn't get arrested (and almost singlehandedly spearheading the resusci-

James Agee

tation of HARRY LANGDON's reputation) and loosing zingers in print back when PAULINE KAEL was still vaguely girlish. (On *Random Harvest*: "I would like to recommend this film to those who can stay interested in Ronald Colman's amnesia for two hours and who could with pleasure eat a bowl of Yardley's shaving soap for breakfast.") Forming a mutual admiration society with John Huston, Agee collaborated with the director on the screenplay for *The African Queen*.

Ai No Corrida. High-toned Japanese skin flick from 1976, featuring actual intercourse, that dragged pornography from the GRINDHOUSE to the art house. Putatively the story of a 1930s brothel servant's affair with the madam's husband, the film legitimized the Snob's furtive desire for smut by allowing him to watch coitus out in the open under the guise of taking in "a study of desire." In the United States, the film carried the repertory-cinema-friendly title *In the Realm of the Senses*, rather than the direct translation, *Bullfight of Love*.

AIP. Commonly used shorthand for American International Pictures, a crank-'em-out production company, founded in 1954, that was among the first institutions to be exalted as a font of Important Kitsch; as far back as 1979, AIP was the subject of an adoring retrospective at the Museum of Modern Art. Unabashedly chasing the whims of fickle teens, AIP's mandate switched from Westerns (ROGER CORMAN's *Apache Woman*) to teen horror (*I Was a Teenage Werewolf*) to Vincent Price's Poe movies (*House of Usher, The Pit and the Pendulum*) to the Annette-and-Frankie Beach Party movies—though, in later years, AIP's output skewed ever more exploitatively toward GRINDHOUSE fare (e.g., PAM GRIER in *Black Mama, White Mama*). *Kutcher exudes the bland hunkiness of a juvenile lead in an old AIP feature.*

Aldrich, Robert. Tough-guy director (1918–83) who, despite his machismo-infused CV (*Kiss Me Deadly, The Dirty Dozen, The Longest Yard*), enjoys unlikely godhead status among Camp Snobs for his two hypermacabre Bette Davis horror-melodramas, *What Ever Happened to Baby Jane?* (1962) and *Hush, Hush, Sweet Charlotte* (1965), which begat a whole movement of using aging female studio-system refugees as clownmakeup grotesques. *Love that lunatic pirouette dance that Bette does with the ice-cream cone at the end of* Baby Jane—*pure, demented Aldrich.*

Almendros, Néstor. Painterly Spanish cinematographer (1930–92) revered by Snobs for his purist's respect for natural light; worked with French New Wavers (ERIC ROHMER, François Truffaut) and American mavericks (MONTE HELLMAN, Martin Scorsese), and, most famously, gave TERRENCE MALICK's *Days of Heaven* the golden-hour glow that camouflaged the film's narrative lapses. *Much as I admire Conrad Hall's work on* In Cold Blood, *I can't help but think that* Néstor Almendros *would have shot it better.*

Altering Eye, The. Must-have Snob book, first published in 1983, that offers a cogent but sawdust-dry analysis of the modernist film movements in Europe and Latin America from ITALIAN NEO-REALISM onward. Long a knapsack staple, the book has now been posted on the Web in its entirety by its author, Robert Kolker, a professor of film studies at the Georgia Institute of Technology.

The Altering Eye

Anger, Kenneth. Hollywood-reared child actor, né Kenneth Anglemyer, turned trash-cinema auteur. Falling under the spell of Aleister Crowley, the suave English occultist, Anger, upon reaching young adulthood, took to making homoerotic, crypto-Fascist shorts such as *Fireworks* (1947) and *Scorpio Rising* (1964)—the latter a locus classicus of gay-biker chic, and a harbinger of Martin Scorsese and Quentin Tarantino in its juxtaposition of jukebox pop and ultraviolence. Still, Anger is best known as the author of *Hollywood Babylon*, his over-amped 1960 compendium of scabrous Tinseltown gossip.

Anime. Catchall term for Japanese or Japanese-style animation, an understanding of which is said by Snobs to be crucial to understanding the future of cinema (yea, of our very culture!), since it, like CHOP-SOCKY, will inform all filmmaking visionaries worth a damn—even though it reliably focuses on species-nonspecific furry animals and childlike humanoids with enormous, saucery eyes. A societal subculture as much as it is a genre, anime takes many forms, including merchandise-shifting product (*Pokémon*), lyrical children's fare (the films of Hayao Miyazaki), and explicit pornography (the subgenre known as *hentai*, in which the childlike humanoids have enormous, R. Crumb–inspired bosoms to go with their enormous, saucery eyes). Anime has established an American beachhead with the Chicago-based Manga Entertainment (*manga* is the Japanese word for comics), the distributor behind the cult hits *Ghost in the Shell* and *Blood: The Last Vampire.*

Antihero. Film-crit term, borrowed from comp-lit studies, that achieved hypercurrency in the late 1960s and '70s when the *EASY RIDERS, RAGING BULLS* generation took wing, its auteurs constructing their films around morally compromised, usually runty, usually ethnic protagonists—such as Robert De Niro's Travis Bickle in *Taxi Driver*, Al Pacino's eponymous character in *Serpico*, and Dustin Hoffman's Ratso Rizzo in *Midnight Cowboy. Vincent Gallo hustles and skitters like a real-life embodiment of a Scorsese* antihero.

Antonioni, Michelangelo. Art-film director regarded, despite his age (he was born in 1912), as a sort of Italian auxiliary to the FRENCH NEW WAVE because of his audacious, conventional-narrative-shunning early-sixties trilogy, *L'Avventura, La Notte,* and *L'Eclisse.* For all the critical kvelling that these MEDITATIONS ON "aliention" and "disaffection" produced, it was Antonioni's English-language debut, 1966's *Blow-Up*, that earned him a gilt pedestal in the Snob pantheon, with its *Austin Powers*–inspiring Swinging London–photographer ANTIHERO, dolly-bird sex romps, Yardbirds-concert interlude, unresolved intrigue over a possible murder, and opening and closing scenes in which Antonioni, in his pursuit of profundity, actually deployed an unexplained gaggle of mimes. Regarded in some Snob circles as a painterly, betwitching allegory on the illusory nature of modern life and in other circles as a full-on con (PAULINE KAEL wrote that old-timers like Ben Hecht banged out satirical comedies about vain, greedy jerks "that said most of what Antonioni does and more, and were entertaining besides"), *Blow-Up* was followed by two more English-language Snob causes célèbres— the train-wreck sixties-activist-tumult movie *Zabriskie Point* (1970) and the artiest Jack Nicholson movie ever made, *The Passenger* (1975).

Apparatus. Comically obtuse blather-term used in semiotics-driven film studies to denote both the camera and the "cinematic system of meaning"; stubbornly used by semioticians as if in fear that they'll be reamed with a cattle prod if the words *camera* or *narrative* pass through their lips. *In its relentless voyeurism and implied violence, Michael Powell's* Peeping Tom *makes deft use of the* apparatus *to signify the male gaze.*

Argento, Asia. Tattooed sexpot Italian actress, incapable of keeping her clothes on, who, perhaps by dint of being the daughter of DARIO ARGENTO, has managed to position herself as an art-damaged alternaauteuress rather than a mere soft-core goth girl. Having directed and starred in such brutal, sex-filled features as *Scarlet Diva* (2000) and *The Heart Is Deceitful Above All Things* (2004), Argento has also dipped a toe into the mainstream, appearing, to rapturous Snob response, in the Vin Diesel vehicle *XXX* (2002).

Argento, Dario. Italian horrormeister who forsook his legitimate screenwriting background (he cowrote Sergio Leone's *Once Upon a Time in the West*) to popularize a genre of splatter pic, known in Italy as the *Giallo*, whose films, like those of HERSCHELL GORDON LEWIS, are required viewing for Gore Snobs. His Snob-ratified classic is *Suspiria* (1977).

Dario Argento

Art of the Moving Picture, The. Nearly impenetrable but historically significant book by Illinois poet Vachel Lindsay, originally published in 1915 and upheld by Snobs as the first critical appraisal of movies as a bonafide art form. Though prescient in its anticipation of film's cultural influence ("Edison is the new Gutenberg. He has invented the new printing"), the book's antiquated prose (movies are "artistic photoplays") makes it rough going for all but the most dogged of Snobs, even in the snappy new edition published by the Modern Library with an introduction by STANLEY KAUFFMANN.

Ashby, Hal. Beautiful loser of the *EASY RIDERS, RAG-ING BULLS* auteur pack, a fuzz-faced, genial, doob-smoking late-bloomer who, Snobs bitterly contend, never gets his due alongside Coppola, Scorsese, Lucas, Altman, Friedkin, BOGDANOVICH, et al. A longtime film editor for director Norman Jewison, Ashby came to national attention with his second movie, *Harold and Maude* (1971), starring the wee BUD CORT as a puckish, suspiciously Ashby-like ANTIHERO in love with an elderly woman. Thereafter, Ashby went on an artistic tear, directing *The Last Detail, Shampoo, Bound for Glory, Coming Home,* and *Being There,* and establishing himself as an "actor's director"—a designation that, like the sports term "player's coach," suggests a mixed blessing of amiability and erratic discipline. Increasingly drug-dependent, Ashby floundered in the eighties, making such inferior films as *Lookin' to Get Out* and *The Slugger's Wife* and struggling with completion anxiety, before succumbing to cancer in 1988, a good decade before Revivalist Snobs began to press his case.

Aspect ratio. The ratio between the width and height of the film frame; 1.85:1 is the American widescreen standard. Though once known only within the filmmaking industry and among those who used to be called "AV nerds" in high-school projectionist clubs, the term has become commonplace on DVD sleeves, a reassurance to potential buyers that their DIRECTOR'S CUT version of *Donnie Darko* hasn't been trimmed to fit TV screens. *Don't get that* Assault on Precinct 13 *DVD—they didn't preserve the original* aspect ratio!

Auberjonois, Rene. Lean, often mustachioed character actor who was a member, along with BUD CORT, of Robert Altman's repertory in the director's muddy-brown period, appearing in *M*A*S*H* (as the original Father Mulcahy), *Brewster McCloud,* and *McCabe and Mrs. Miller*—a body of work that makes him a casual name-drop for Snobs, who would just as soon ignore his later fame as the sniffy, officious chief of staff on TV's *Benson* and as the shape-shifting Odo on TV's *Star Trek: Deep Space Nine.*

Auteur theory, the. Immutable tenet of film theory that holds that the director, rather than the screenwriter, producer, or star, is the "author" of a film. First posited by François Truffaut in *CAHIERS DU CINÉMA* in 1954, Americanized by ANDREW SARRIS in *Film Culture* in 1962, and then ridiculed by the gadfly PAULINE KAEL in *Film Quarterly* in 1963, the theory contends that a director's signature style—or "filmic personality," in Snob-speak—is of greater significance than the actual quality of his individual films. Though the debate over the auteur theory's worth subsided long ago, Snobs still brandish the theory to make cases for the greatness of such unworthies as David Fincher.

Bass, Saul. Bronx-born animator, graphic designer, and director (1920–1996) whose strikingly imaginative title sequences introduced dozens of films, including some of the best by Otto Preminger (*Anatomy of a Murder*), Alfred Hitchcock (*Vertigo*), and Martin Scorsese (*Goodfellas*), and, in some cases, were more memorable than the films themselves (Edward Dmytryk's *Walk on the Wild Side*, Scorsese's *Casino*). A Snob controversy rages over the extent of his involvement in *Psycho*'s shower scene—some swear he actually directed it, while others say he just drew the storyboards—and hard-core Bassists extol his sole feature as director, *Phase IV* (1974), an impenetrable sci-fi story about superintelligent ants.

Beery, Wallace. Thickset, Doberman-faced character actor (1885–1949) who found unlikely success as a leading man in late-period silent features and early-period talkies, most notably in *Min and Bill* (1930), a salty harborside slice-of-life tale costarring the equally linebackerish Marie Dressler, and *The Champ* (1931), in which he played the faded-boxer dad of tow-headed Jackie Cooper (winning an Oscar for his efforts). Cherished by Snobs as the embodiment of the sort of "real" mug that old Hollywood embraced before shallow youth culture and Kabbalah took hold, he was paid tribute by the Coen brothers in *Barton Fink* (1991), in which it was the titular character's accursed fate to script a "Wallace Beery wrestling picture."

Wallace Beery

Bogdanovich, Peter. Cinema's foremost callow-Film Snob-turned-auteur until Quentin Tarantino came along. Gaining a foothold in the movie world by writing a MONOGRAPH for the Museum of

Modern Art's Orson Welles retrospective in 1960, when he was only twenty-one, Bogdanovich moved into film criticism for *Esquire*, and, in the mid-1960s, became one of ROGER CORMAN's many protégés, which afforded him the chance to direct his first picture, *Targets* (1968). A dedicated auteurist and treasurer of Hollywood's Depression-era golden age, Bogdanovich scored a massive critical trifecta with *The Last Picture Show* (1971), *What's Up, Doc?* (1972), and *Paper Moon* (1973), all of which convincingly evoked vanished American milieus and were suffused with flagrant MOVIENESS (*What's Up Doc* in particular, with its rat-a-tat echoes of HOWARD HAWKS's screwball films). Bogdanovich's subsequent hubris (along with his dumping of first wife–secret weapon POLLY PLATT for yowsa actress Cybill Shepherd) made him ripe for a nasty comeuppance, and, accordinglly, his next few films flopped, and he never re-gained his momentum. Semi-redeeming himself by be-coming Welles's friend, protector, and official interlocutor in the 1970s (and later publishing a book of their conver-sations, *Directed by Orson Welles*), Bogdanovich has man-aged a series of modest comebacks in his later career, directing *Mask* (1985) and *The Cat's Meow* (2001), and playing Dr. Melfi's psychiatrist on *The Sopranos*.

Bollywood. Broad term for India's Bombay-based film industry, which, though it has produced visionaries like Raj Kapoor, more routinely pumps out soapy, mass-market movies that, when projected in theaters in American university towns, somehow morph into art films.

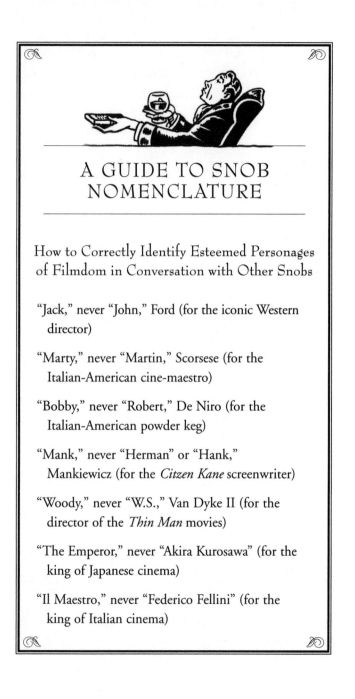

A GUIDE TO SNOB NOMENCLATURE

How to Correctly Identify Esteemed Personages of Filmdom in Conversation with Other Snobs

"Jack," never "John," Ford (for the iconic Western director)

"Marty," never "Martin," Scorsese (for the Italian-American cine-maestro)

"Bobby," never "Robert," De Niro (for the Italian-American powder keg)

"Mank," never "Herman" or "Hank," Mankiewicz (for the *Citzen Kane* screenwriter)

"Woody," never "W.S.," Van Dyke II (for the director of the *Thin Man* movies)

"The Emperor," never "Akira Kurosawa" (for the king of Japanese cinema)

"Il Maestro," never "Federico Fellini" (for the king of Italian cinema)

Brakhage, Stan. Prolific, Kansas City–born maker of labor-intensive films known only to difficult art-world people; the proto–Matthew Barney. Starting in the 1950s, Brakhage made more than 300 films using various methodologies—sometimes hand-painting the celluloid frame by frame, sometimes filming actual scenes of childbirth, autopsy, and intercourse in a Warholian deadpan. Was accorded the honor of being anthologized by the CRITERION COLLECTION not long before his 2004 death. Titles include *Thigh Line Lyre Triangular, Christ Mass Sex Dance,* and *The Cat of the Worm's Green Realm.*

 Cahiers du Cinéma. The single greatest force in inviting ridicule of French intellectuals as absurdist twits. Founded in 1951, the still-extant Paris-based monthly first attracted significant American attention when, in 1954, it published contributor François Truffaut's AUTEUR THEORY. Subsequent issues built auteurist mythologies around such red-blooded Americans as DON SIEGEL, SAMUEL FULLER, and NICHOLAS RAY, putting far more thought into analysis of these directors' B pictures than the directors had put into making them. *Cahiers du Cinéma* also abetted the French mania for Jerry Lewis, deeming him "le Roi du Crazy."

Campbell, Bruce. Jut-jawed cult actor whose reputation rests on his appearance in SAM RAIMI's *Evil Dead* movies and his cameos in Coen brothers films. (Campbell roomed with the Coens and Raimi in their prefame days of the 1980s.) Though dependably employed today on television and as a voice-over specialist for video games, he is better appreciated by Snobs for such under-the-radar schlock-SPLOITATION flicks as *Bubba Ho-tep* (2002), in which he was perfectly cast as an elderly Elvis Presley.

Cassavetes, John. Handsome actor-director (1929–89) whose heavily improvised, occasionally tedious independent films, especially *Faces* (1968) and *Husbands* (1970), anticipated and influenced the DOGME 95 movement—though Cassavetes carried off his self-indulgences with an acuity and slim-lapelled flair that his heirs lack.

John
Cassavetes

Cassel, Seymour. Rumpled, mustachioed character actor who made his name as part of JOHN CASSAVETES's repertory in such films as *Too Late Blues, Faces,* and *Minnie and Moskowitz*—and, as such, has been deployed in his later career by such hip-minded directors as Wes Anderson, Alexandre Rockwell, and Steve Buscemi, often as a plaid-jacketed scamster type.

Cazale, John. Wiry, sympathetic ethno-character actor of receding hairline and small but impeccable filmmography—all five of his films (the first two *Godfather* movies, *The Conversation, Dog Day Afternoon,* and *The Deer Hunter*) were Oscar-nominated for Best Picture. An unsung hero of the *EASY RIDERS, RAGING BULLS* era, Cazale, best known for playing Fredo, the dim-bulb middle Corleone brother (between James Caan's hotheaded Sonny and Al Pacino's icy-veined Michael), was sufficiently charismatic to have bedazzled the young, then unapproachably Aryan Meryl Streep on the set of *The Deer Hunter.* He and Streep were engaged to be married when he succumbed to bone cancer in 1978, when he was just forty-two.

Chop-socky. Formerly derogatory term for Asian martial-arts movies, since repurposed, à la "queer," as the hipster's term of choice. Though it encompasses everything from sixties-era Taiwanese kung fu films to Bruce Lee's pan-Pacific hits of the early seventies, chop-socky is most identified with the latter-day Hong Kong film industry that begat Jackie Chan,

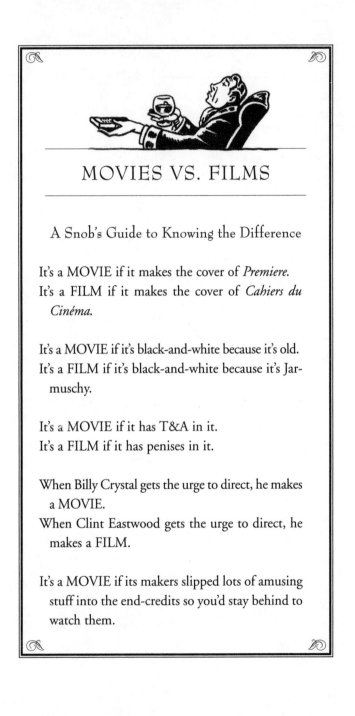

MOVIES VS. FILMS

A Snob's Guide to Knowing the Difference

It's a MOVIE if it makes the cover of *Premiere*.
It's a FILM if it makes the cover of *Cahiers du Cinéma*.

It's a MOVIE if it's black-and-white because it's old.
It's a FILM if it's black-and-white because it's Jarmuschy.

It's a MOVIE if it has T&A in it.
It's a FILM if it has penises in it.

When Billy Crystal gets the urge to direct, he makes a MOVIE.
When Clint Eastwood gets the urge to direct, he makes a FILM.

It's a MOVIE if its makers slipped lots of amusing stuff into the end-credits so you'd stay behind to watch them.

It's a FILM if its end-credits are normal, boring end-credits, but everyone around you stays to watch them anyway.

Bruce Willis, a MOVIE guy, gained FILM credibility by being in *Pulp Fiction*. Steve Buscemi, a FILM guy, gained MOVIE credibility by being in *Armageddon*.

It's a MOVIE if there are black people in it, unless the black person is Forest Whitaker or Jeffrey Wright.
It's a FILM if there are Asian people in it, unless the Asian person is Jackie Chan or Jet Li.

A John Grisham novel becomes a crappy MOVIE.
A Gabriel García Márquez novel becomes a crappy FILM.

It's a MOVIE if its male lead is hurled through plate glass.
It's a FILM if its male lead has sexual urgings for young boys, his sister, or his mother.

The Coen brothers are MOVIE buffs who make FILMS.

> It's a MOVIE if it's preceded by a trailer for the latest Jerry Bruckheimer epic.
>
> It's a FILM if it's preceded by an announcement from a pear-shaped, balding man down in front who identifies himself as "Michael, the programming director."
>
> It's a FILM if it's from the Indian subcontinent, even if the people in the Indian subcontinent think it's a MOVIE.
>
> Tom Waits will never, ever star in a MOVIE.
> Tom Hanks will never, ever star in a FILM.

Chow Yun-Fat, and John Woo. Despite genre limitations that its Asian audiences plainly recognize, chopsocky, like ANIME, is upheld by feverish Snobs as the path all future cinema must take, which is why the only recent mainstream films that have mattered are *Crouching Tiger, Hidden Dragon*, the *Matrix* trilogy, and Quentin Tarantino's *Kill Bill* movies. *Tarantino's a Johnny-come-lately; I was going down to Chinatown for my* chop-socky *fix in '83!*

Cinecittà. Massive filmmaking complex located outside of Rome, best known as the place where Fellini shot most of his films and where U.S. studios, seeking to lower production costs, steered their business in the wide-screen era of *Quo Vadis, Ben-Hur,* and *Cleopatra.* For Snobs, the ability to pronounce "Cinecittà" (Chee-nih-chee-TAH) is a crucial demarcator between the savant and the idiot.

Cinefile. The premier Film Snob video shop in Los Angeles (located on Santa Monica Boulevard off Sawtelle), specializing in obscure DVDs and out-of-print videos; where embittered would-be Quentins go to rent extremely rare super-8 kung fu pix and old DOLEMITE movies.

Clift, Montgomery. Fragile, doomed matinee idol (1920–66), posthumously adopted by hipsters and queer theorists on account of his pansexual appeal, intense performances, open-secret homosexuality, and tragic final years. (Both the Clash and R.E.M. devoted songs to him, "The Right Profile" and "Monty Got a Raw Deal," respectively.) An instant star opposite John Wayne in HOWARD HAWKS's Western *Red River* (1948), Clift quickly established himself as a sort of proto-ANTI-HERO, racking up three Oscar nominations in five years for *The Search* (1948), *A Place in the Sun* (1951), and *From Here to Eternity* (1953). In 1957, he was badly disfigured in a car accident after leaving a party, surviving when his friend Elizabeth Taylor rushed to the scene and dislodged two teeth from his throat. After reconstructive facial surgery, Clift returned to the screen more mesmerizingly

Montgomery Clift

damaged than ever, starring opposite Taylor in JOSEPH L. MANKIEWICZ's adaptation of Tennessee Williams's gothic weird-out play *Suddenly Last Summer* and as Sigmund Freud in John Huston's *Freud* (1962). But pill-popping, alcoholism, and mental illness claimed Clift in 1966, at the age of forty-five, just as he was on the verge of reuniting with Taylor in Huston's acutely bizarro MEDI-TATION ON homosexuality and repression, *Reflections in a Golden Eye* (1967); Marlon Brando ably stepped into Clift's role.

Cocksucker Blues. Warts-and-all documentary of the Rolling Stones' 1972 tour, directed by photographer Robert Frank and celebrated by both Film and Rock Snobs for being very difficult to see; the Stones, having second thoughts about being captured in all their *Exile on Main Street*–era debauchery, obtained a court injunction against the film's distribution, ultimately striking an odd deal with Frank in which *Cocksucker Blues* can only be screened once a year, with the director present. Reputed to be rife with illicit orgy scenes and appalling drug abuse, the grainy, low-production-values movie is actually rather tame by today's standards, but still entertaining as an archival curio, especially in its unintentionally funny scenes depicting Bianca Jagger's existential ennui.

Corman, Roger. Improbably patrician, mild-mannered purveyor of schlock and avuncular mentor to some of Hollywood's most combustible, provocative directors. Stanford- and Harvard-educated,

Corman forsook a career as a literary agent to become a director for AIP in the 1950s and '60s, churning out dirt-cheap genre flicks with Henry Ford efficiency. As a producer, he discovered Jack Nicholson and served as an employer-sage to such future auteurs as Francis Ford Coppola, MONTE HELLMAN, PETER BOG-DANOVICH, John Sayles, and Jonathan Demme, some of whom repaid him with wink-wink cameos (Corman played a senator in Coppola's *The Godfather, Part II*, and the FBI chief in Demme's *The Silence of the Lambs*). With his brother, Gene, Corman founded his own production company, New World Pictures, in 1970, which served the dual purpose of churning out trash-SPLOITATION pics (including the best-known WIP, or women-in-prison, films) and distributing such Eurofare as Bergman's *Cries and Whispers* and Fellini's *Amarcord* to U.S. art houses.

Cort, Bud. Gnomish character actor who, during a dizzying period in 1970–71, emerged as one of that auteur-choked era's most unlikely ANTIHEROes, playing the title role in Robert Altman's *Brewster McCloud*, the colead in ROGER CORMAN's *Gas-s-s-s*, and Harold, the youngster who falls for a little old lady, in HAL ASHBY's *Harold and Maude*. A disfiguring, MONTGOMERY CLIFT–evocative car accident in the late seventies took years away from his career, but Cort re-cently reemerged in Wes Anderson's *The Life Aquatic with Steve Zissou*

Bud Cort

(2004), portending a SEYMOUR CASSEL–like late-period career in the films of homagist directors.

Criterion Collection, the. Achingly tasteful video-reissue company that, like the Rock Snob–beloved labels Rhino and Sundazed, has found success by recycling old movies as lavish, extras-laden packages for deep-pocketed connoisseurs. (The two-disc Criterion version of *Straw Dogs*, for example, comes in Dolby Digital Stereo 2.0, with a full-length SAM PECKINPAH documentary and a new interview with Susan George.) Having all but cornered the market on the works of prestige directors like Jean Cocteau, Federico Fellini, and Akira Kurosawa, Criterion has branched out into repackaging rock documentaries (*Gimme Shelter, Monterey Pop*) and "acceptable" fun movies such as *My Man Godfrey, Armageddon,* and *Withnail and I.*

Cronenberg, David. Cheerfully depraved Canadian horror auteur whose dystopian weird-out flicks *Scanners* (1981) and *Videodrome* (1983) enchanted Splatter Snobs immediately (both films feature heads exploding) but repulsed critics; Roger Ebert called the latter film "one of the least entertaining films ever made." After a late-eighties period of flirtation with the mainstream and critical approval (*The Fly, Dead Ringers*), Cronenberg returned to his gloppy, fleshy, violent roots and his core Snob constituency, bravely adapting books previously perceived to be unfilmable, William S. Burroughs's

Naked Lunch and J. G. Ballard's *Crash. The Wachowskis don't have nothin' on* Cronenberg; *he was pulling that alternate-reality shit back in the day!*

Decalogue, The. Ambitious but not wholly endurable series of ten 55-minute films, produced for Polish television in the late 1980s by director Kryztof Kieslowski, the themed-series-mad auteur also behind the *Trois Couleurs* triptych (*Bleu, Blanc, Rouge*) of the early 1990s. Each *Decalogue* film deals obliquely with one of the Ten Commandments, albeit in the drab setting of a Polish housing project. The FACETS VIDEO box set of *The Decalogue* is a reliable Snob fetish object/stocking stuffer.

Deep focus. Fetishized cinematographic technique that enables all the action in a shot, from the foreground to the deep background, to remain sharply defined. Employed most famously in *Citizen Kane* and robustly championed by the French cinephile and theorist André Bazin. *Hou Hsiao-Hsien's graceful use of* deep focus *recalls the work of Yasujiro Ozu, non?*

De Palma, Brian. Newark-born director with powerful ability to polarize Snobs, some dismissing him as a hack Hitchcock homagist and others fulsomely praising his masterfully vulgar thrillers—such as *Sisters* (1973), *Blow Out* (1981), *Raising Cain* (1992), and *Femme Fatale* (2002)—as the apex of cinema, awesome in their preposterous plots, giddy camerawork, doppelgänger motifs, hot babes, and prodigious use of slo-mo. (*CAHIERS DU CINÉMA* rated De Palma's *Carlito's Way*, from 1993, as the best film of the nineties.) What all Snobs agree upon is that his mainstream, moneymaking flicks—such as *The Untouchables, Mission: Impossible*, and even the behemothic pop-culture reference point *Scarface*—do not merit serious consideration.

Deren, Maya. Sulkily beautiful experimental filmmaker (1917–61), renowned among Art Snobs for such surrealistic shorts as *Meshes of the Afternoon* (1943), which has no soundtrack but for a drumbeat that accompanies Deren's movements as she wields a knife at no one in particular and encounters an unexplained hooded figure wearing a reflective mask. Born Eleanora Derenkowsky and raised in New York after her Jewish family fled the pogroms in their native Ukraine, Deren quickly insinuated herself into the American film, dance, and difficult-art worlds, using a Guggenheim fellowship to study Haitian voodoo, and becoming a voodoo priestess in the process. Even STAN BRAKHAGE thought her stuff was weird. *David Lynch's dislocated narratives in* Mulholland Drive *and* Lost Highway *have* Maya Deren's *influence written all over them.*

Maya Deren

De Vol, Frank. Musician and soundtrack composer (1911–99) whose futura-luxe onscreen credit in 1950s and '60s movies, "Music by De Vol"—suggesting a sleek, avocado-green pushbutton incidental-music generator—endears him to Kitsch Snobs. A radio bandleader in the forties, De Vol was tapped to work in movies, appropriately enough, by kitschmeister ROBERT ALDRICH, moving on to compose the "groovy" scores of such films as *Pillow Talk* (1959), *Under the Yum Yum Tree* (1963), and *Guess Who's Coming to Dinner?* (1967), as well as the theme song for *The Brady Bunch.* Not without a sense of humor about his peculiar niche, he played the bandleader Happy Kyne on Martin Mull's subversive seventies talk-show send-up *Fernwood 2 Nite.*

Diegesis. Unnecessarily opaque film-studies term for the world inhabited by a film's characters; the music playing on a character's radio, for example, is diegetic sound, whereas the ominous music foreshadowing the character's graphic decapitation is nondiegetic sound. *The* diegesis *of* Last Year at Marienbad *is deliberately ambiguous, not unlike that of* Bill and Ted's Bogus Journey.

Director's cut. A version of a film that contains different scenes and editing from the version that saw original theatrical release, compiled postrelease by the film's director or his faithful acolytes—usually to redress what is perceived to be a studio's bottom-line–minded butchery of a masterpiece, though sometimes simply to satisfy the filmmaker's itch to tweak. The earliest director's cuts were rare, unexpurgated prints shown at repertory cinemas—such as the four-hour cut of SAM PECKIN-

PAH's *The Wild Bunch* rescued from obscurity in 1974 by Jerry Harvey, later the excitable Snob programmer for L.A.'s Z CHANNEL. But in 1980, Steven Spielberg won wide release for his "Special Edition" of *Close Encounters of the Third Kind* (featuring new footage inside the alien mothership), just three years after the apparently unspecial original had come out, paving the way for a slew of told-you-so directorial do-overs, such as the gigantosaurus rerelease of Sergio Leone's 1984 Jewish-gangster epic *Once Upon a Time in America*, which nearly doubled the original U.S. release's 139-minute length. With the advent of the VHS and DVD eras, the artistic justifications for a director's cut were superseded, ironically, by the bottom-line–mindedness of the studios, who now needed "new" content to sell videos. As such, even *Nutty Professor II: The Klumps* has received the reverent director's-cut treatment.

Doc Films. The film society of the University of Chicago, founded in 1932 as the Documentary Film Group. Hard-core beyond words and lay comprehension, the society is populated by nineteen-year-olds who have already seen every film ever made, and boasts its own Dolby Digital–equipped cinema and an impressive roster of alumni that includes Snob-revered critic DAVE KEHR.

Dogme 95. Severe, self-parodying directors' collective (founded by the Danish filmmakers Lars von Trier and Thomas Vinterberg in 1995) that calls for greater authen-

D

ticity in film and argues that new video technology will democratize the filmmaking process and deliver the masses from their oppression by evil, formulaic, special effects–laden studio fare. Dogme 95 makes its members adhere to a "Vow of Chastity," the ten rules of which include "The camera must be handheld" and "The film must not contain superficial action. (Murders, weapons, etc. must not occur.)" Official Dogme films are amusingly numbered and titled like abstract-art studies— e.g., *Dogme #2: Idioterne, Dogme #8: Fuckland.*

Dolemite. Cinematic alter ego of Rudy Ray Moore, a pudgy, vainglorious stand-up comic who established his own subgenre within the 1970s blaxploitation movement. The title character of his Dolemite films was a foul-mouthed, cunnilingus-obsessed lady-killer in pimp attire who annihilated his nemeses with kung-fu moves and withering jive and compulsorily revealed his large buttocks in sex scenes. An unusual crossover figure, Moore is hailed by both melanin-deficient trash-film geeks and hip-hoppers such as Ice-T and Snoop Dogg, who consider him an influence on gangsta rap.

Dolemite

Downey Sr., Robert. Hippie-cinema stalwart and father of likable, albeit frequently indisposed, namesake actor. The senior Downey specialized in whacked-out sociopolitical satires suffused with stoner mischievism—*Putney Swope* (1969) depicted a black militant's accidental appointment as head of a Madison Avenue ad agency, while *Greaser's Palace* (1972) was a Christ parable centered on a Wild West song-and-dance man. Though these films, like so much cinema of lysergic vintage, are now borderline unwatchable, they remain viable as Snob name-drops.

Ealing Studios. English film company best known for its clipped, clever-clever comedies of the late 1940s and early '50s, many of which (*Kind Hearts and Coronets, The Lavender Hill Mob, The Ladykillers*) starred Alec Guinness. In their drollery and amphetamine-quick pacing and dialogue, Ealing comedies prefigured and directly influenced the Beatles and Monty Python. In 1988, an indebted John Cleese exhumed the elderly Ealing director Charles Crichton to direct *A Fish Called Wanda*.

Easy Riders, Raging Bulls. Landmark 1999 history of the so-called American New Wave filmmakers of the late 1960s and '70s, written by Gene Shalit–lookalike journalist Peter Biskind. Interweaving the narratives of the denimy, sideburned mavericks who bucked the crumbling, top-heavy studio system by making inexpensive, idiosyncratic films—many of them influenced by the FRENCH NEW WAVE and mentor ROGER CORMAN's quick 'n' cheap ways— the book was an instant industry and Snob must-read upon its publication, not least because of the prurient details it revealed about the drug-taking and sexual proclivities of such figures as DENNIS HOPPER, Peter Fonda, Francis Ford Coppola, Martin Scorsese, Steven Spielberg, George Lucas, Margot Kidder (who sunbathed nude!), Robert Towne, and HAL ASHBY. Though many of these figures have registered their displeasure with their portrayals—with PETER BOG-DANOVICH and William Friedkin coming off as particularly hubristic and asshole-ish—*Easy Riders, Raging Bulls* has actually served to cement their legends and preserve their names for posterity, lending them a collective identity that the term "American New Wave" never quite explained.

Egoyan, Atom. Cairo-born, Toronto-based, ethnic-Armenian director who ranks even above DAVID CRONENBERG and GUY MADDIN as the Great White North's most Snob-ratified auteur. His earlier films, such as *Next of Kin* (1984), *Family Viewing* (1987), and *The Adjuster* (1991), were detached, heavy-meta exercises that frequently found Egoyan's characters wielding video cameras, watching videotape, and revealing their sexual obsessions, thereby making his work extremely hospitable to film theorists and their standby "dissociation" and "voyeurism" tropes. More recently, Egoyan has warmed up somewhat with *The Sweet Here-after* (1997), his justly celebrated schoolbus-full-of-kids-falling-through-the-ice picture, and *Ararat* (2002), which uses his film-within-a-film technique not to reflect "the consciousness of the gaze" but to examine the history of discrimination against Armenians.

THE SNOB CHEAT SHEET
FOR CONFUSING
SIMILARITIES

Bibi Andersson is the Swedish actress who appeared in several of Ingmar Bergman's most famous films, including *Smiles of a Summer Night, The Seventh Seal, Wild Strawberries,* and *Persona*. **Harriet Andersson** is the Swedish actress who appeared in several of Ingmar Bergman's *other* famous films, such as *Through a Glass Darkly, Cries and Whispers,* and *Fanny and Alexander,* not to mention *Smiles of a Summer Night* and Lars von Trier's *Dogville*. Bibi and Harriet are not related.

Cléo from 5 to 7 is a dreamy sixties film about two uncertain hours in the life of a pop singer, directed by the French New Waver Agnès Varda. *Chloe in the Afternoon* is a breezy seventies film about uncertainty in the life of a horny married man, directed by the French New Waver Eric Rohmer.

Van Heflin was the rugged, pug-faced MGM studio player who appeared in *The Prowler, Shane,* and other movies of the 1940s and '50s. **Van Johnson** was the scrubbed, baby-faced MGM player who appeared in *State of the Union, The Caine Mutiny,* and other movies of the 1940s and '50s. **Val Lewton** was the Russian-born producer best known for such spooky RKO films as *Cat People, The Seventh Victim,* and *I Walked with a Zombie.*

Josef von Sternberg was a diminutive, Vienna-born director who added "von" to his name as an affectation and made several films in the 1930s starring Marlene Dietrich, his then lover, including *The Blue Angel, Morocco, Shanghai Express,* and *The Scarlet Empress.* **Erich von Stroheim** was a diminutive, Vienna-born director who added "von" to his name as an affectation and made the important silent films *Foolish Wives, Greed,* and *The Wedding March* in the 1920s, later making memorable appearances as an actor in *Grand Illusion* and *Sunset Boulevard.*

Sidney Lumet is the intense director of such gritty slices of New York City realism as *Serpico, Dog Day Afternoon,* and *Prince of the City.* **Syd-**

ney Pollack is the affable director of such populist, Academy-pleasing fare as *The Way We Were, Tootsie,* and *Out of Africa.*

William Wyler was the exacting, demanding director who made waves in the 1930s with his films *Dodsworth* and *Jezebel,* and drew on his World War II experiences as a member of the U.S. Army Air Corps to make the war films *Mrs. Miniver* and *The Best Years of Our Lives.* **William Wellman** was the exacting, demanding director who made waves in the 1930s with his films *The Public Enemy* and *A Star Is Born,* and drew on his World War I experiences as a decorated pilot for the French Foreign Legion to make the war films *The Story of G.I. Joe* and *Battleground.*

Howard Hawks was the alliteratively named filmmaker who directed Cary Grant movies in his younger days (*Bringing Up Baby, His Girl Friday*), and, later on, wound up directing such gigantic Westerns as *Red River, The Big Sky, Rio Bravo,* and *Rio Lobo.* **Henry Hathaway** was the alliteratively named filmmaker who directed Gary Cooper films in his younger days (*The Lives of a Bengal Dancer, Peter Ibbetson*), and, later on, wound up directing such gigantic Westerns as *Rawhide, Nevada Smith,* and *True Grit.*

Estelle Parsons is the actress best known for playing Clyde Barrow's jumpy sister-in-law in *Bonnie and Clyde.* **Louella Parsons** was a powerful Hollywood gossip columnist syndicated in the newspapers of William Randolph Hearst.

Paul Verhoeven is the Dutch director of such violent, mordantly humorous films as *Robocop, Basic Instinct,* and *Starship Troopers.* **Michael Verhoeven** is the German director of the mordantly humorous true-story film *The Nasty Girl.*

The Trouble with Harry is a lesser-known Hitchcock movie released in 1955, about the comic consequences of the discovery of a corpse in a small New England town. *The Plot Against Harry* is an obscure comedy—directed by Michael Roemer in 1969, and concerning the travails of a baleful Jewish ex-con—that wasn't actually released until 1989, when it won raves as a time-capsule period piece in art houses.

Anita Ekberg is the pneumatic Swedish bombshell who charmed Marcello Mastroianni in *La*

Dolce Vita. **Britt Ekland** is the pneumatic Swedish bombshell who married Peter Sellers, dated Rod Stewart, and appeared in *Get Carter* and *The Wicker Man*. **Elke Sommer** is the pneumatic German bombshell who appeared opposite Peter Sellers in *A Shot in the Dark*.

William Goldman is a high-priced veteran screenwriter who has won Oscars for the screenplays of *Butch Cassidy and the Sundance Kid* and *All the President's Men,* and who is an in-demand script doctor, notable for having done a polish on *Last Action Hero*. **Bo Goldman** is a high-priced veteran screenwriter who has won Oscars for the screenplays of *One Flew Over the Cuckoo's Nest* and *Melvin and Howard,* and who is an in-demand script doctor, notable for having done a polish on *The Flamingo Kid*.

Evans, Robert. Compellingly reptilian film producer who, as the Vitalis-coiffed head of production at Paramount Pictures in the late 1960s and early '70s, presided over the *EASY RIDERS, RAGING BULLS* revolution in American cinema, overseeing the *Godfather* pictures and *Chinatown,* among other classics. A precipitous fall from grace in the 1980s (a cocaine bust, a link to a murder case, a spotty record as an independent producer, an ever more frightening array of tinted eyeglasses) set the stage for his comeback in the 1990s as a cuddly Hollywood survivor and found-object source of amusement and adulation from hipster industry youths. His raffish I-did-it-my-way 1994 memoir, *The Kid Stays in the Picture*, became a hit, particularly in its audio format, read by Evans himself in a slurred basso, paving the way for a successful 2002 film adaptation of the book and a short-lived cartoon series on Comedy Central (*Kid Notorious*, 2003).

Facets Video. Comprehensively stocked video shop in Film Snob–choked Chicago, renowned nationwide for its array of foreign titles and Francophile pretensions; it prefers to be known as a "videothèque," not a store, and its adjunct theater—which offers "cinechats" with such visiting directors as GUY MADDIN and PETER GREENAWAY—is called a "cinémathèque." Arguably the only video shop with a self-imposed mandate to turn impressionable children into Film Snobs, Facets offers a Future Filmmakers Membership that allows kids to borrow such titles as *City Lights* and *Silas Marner* for free.

Falconetti, Maria. French stage actress of the early twentieth century, renowned for having given only two film performances, the more significant of which was in the title role of the Snob urtext *The Passion of Joan of Arc* (1928). A *FILM COMMENT* writer tried to stump the Oracle of Bacon at Virginia Web site—which runs a computer program that plays the Six Degrees of Kevin Bacon game—by entering Falconetti's name, only to find that, despite her scant film credits, she could be connected to Bacon in just three steps.

Farber, Manny. Beloved *alter kocker* film critic emeritus, now working as a painter in Southern California. Preceding his friend PAULINE KAEL by more than a decade as a nonconformist thinker about movies, Farber got his start writing reviews for *The New Republic* in the 1940s and proved as comfortable deconstructing Tex Avery cartoons and DON SIEGEL genre exercises as he was evaluating the French New Wave and Rainer

Manny Farber

Werner Fassbinder—in effect, inventing the prevailing critical vogue for high thought on low entertainment. A big influence on Snob-revered critic JONATHAN ROSENBAUM, Farber, more than Kael or ANDREW SARRIS, is the name to drop for instant Crit Snob credibility.

Fessenden, Larry. Gaunt, raggedy character actor turned hotly tipped savior of indie horror. Having written and directed the vampire movie *Habit* (1997) and the creepfest *Wendigo* (2001), Fessenden bears the weight of Snob expectation that he will eventually deliver some sort of horror masterwork that will place him in

Larry Fessenden

league with John Carpenter, George Romero, DARIO ARGENTO, and seventies-era BRIAN DE PALMA.

Film Comment. Smug, aggressively elitist bimonthly magazine published by the Film Society of Lincoln Center. Where Snobs go to read (or write) dithery articles about BOLLYWOOD and despairing critiques of popular cinema.

Film Threat. Surprisingly buoyant, unsmug Web 'zine (originally a print magazine) devoted to independent film. Where Snobs go to read fulsome appreciations of Sam Raimi and interviews with such Queens of the B's as Debbie Rochon and Tina Krause.

Flaming Creatures. The most incendiary of the trash films of Jack Smith, an underground camp-queen filmmaker (his other titles included *I Was a Male Yvonne DeCarlo* and *Brassieres of Atlantis*) who is upheld, like the KUCHAR BROTHERS, as an undercredited influence on the likes of Andy Warhol and John Waters. Filmed in 1962 for about $300, on stock that Smith had shoplifted, *Flaming Creatures* features a parade of trannies, hermaphrodites, exposed genitalia, and saggy bosoms against a cheapo *Arabian Nights* backdrop, and caused such a ruckus upon its release (with Federico Fellini hailing it as a masterpiece and Strom Thurmond denouncing it in Washington, D.C.) that Smith, emotionally exhausted, withdrew from filmmaking. He died in 1989 of HIV-related illness at the age of fifty-six.

4:30 Movie, The. Seminal afternoon movie broadcast on Channel 7, ABC-TV's local New York affiliate, in the 1970s. With its themed weeks devoted to cheapo genres (such as Japanese monster movies, ROGER CORMAN's Edgar Allan Poe movies, and RAY HARRYHAUSEN's *Sinbad* epics), *The 4:30 Movie* influenced a great number of the New York metro area's filmmakers of tomorrow, giving them a crash course in trash film and preparing them for their graduation to DAVID CRONENBERG films. The program was also remembered for its propulsive theme song and post-psychedelic opening animation of a silhouetted camera-man operating a whirring machine.

Freaks. Genuinely aberrant studio film from 1932, directed by Tod Browning for MGM, that featured mal-formed sideshow folk (including pinheads, Siamese twins, and an armless, legless man known as "the Living Torso") as the cast in a plotline about a traveling circus whose comely trapeze artist meanly manipulates an amorous midget, only to get her gruesome comeup-pance. Renowned among cultural-studies dorks for the number of "pop" references it produced, including the Ramones' "Gabba gabba hey!" cry (an approximation of the affronted freaks' chant) and Bill Griffith's *Zippy the Pinhead* cartoon character (based in part on Schlitze, the male pinhead who padded around in a housedress).

French New Wave. Influential cinematic movement, circa 1958–64, in which a group of young French directors, most of them contributors to *CAHIERS DU CINÉMA*, rebelled against the stuffy traditions of their forebears by making and celebrating films bearing a personal style as defined by the AUTEUR THEORY. New Wavers Claude Chabrol, François Truffaut, Jean-Luc Godard, Jacques Rivette, and ERIC ROHMER threw themselves into micro-budget productions of their own scripts, with Truffaut's *The 400 Blows* (1959) and Godard's *Breathless* (1960) filling up art houses even in the United States. The French New Wave clearly inspired Arthur Penn's *Bonnie and Clyde* (1967) and the whole *EASY RIDERS, RAGING BULLS* revolution that came in its wake (Steven Spielberg would honor Truffaut by casting him in *Close Encounters of the Third Kind*), and the movement's influence is palpable still in such sexy, fresh films as Alfonso Cuarón's *Y Tu Mama También*; such experimental, difficult films as Mike Figgis's *Timecode*; and in such such sexy, fresh, experimental, difficult films as Wong Kar-Wai's *Fallen Angels*.

Fuller, Samuel. Grizzled, irascible, ultraprolific director and ex–crime reporter (1911–97) who defined the first era of independent film with his violent pulp pictures in the 1950s and '60s. Though his Snob repute is unimpeachable, many Film Snobs would be hard-pressed to actually name one of his films. (His eighties comeback movies, *The Big Red One* and *White Dog*, are the fallbacks.) In the latter part of his life, he relocated to France and basked in his auteur status there.

German Expressionism. Multimedia post–World War I artistic movement whose film arm specialized in spooky, histrionic, atmospheric horror flicks—such as Robert Wiene's *The Cabinet of Doctor Caligari*, Fritz Lang's *M,* and F. W. Murnau's *Nosferatu*—that, despite the heavy sanctity with which they're treated by Snobs, are actually entertaining. German Expressionism was a huge influence on film noir in its use of shadow and light, and on Tim Burton in its grotesquerie, revelry in artifice, and general MOVIENESS.

Goldstein, Bruce. Lovable-mensch head of repertory programming for Film Forum, home of New York City's premier revival screen, and founder of Rialto Pictures, a company that imports and restores foreign classics (such as Carol Reed's *The Third Man* and Federico Fellini's *Nights of Cabiria*) to their rightful DIRECTOR'S CUT fullness and print quality, sometimes for theatrical rerelease, and other times for DVD release via the CRITERION COLLECTION. A Long Island baby boomer, Goldstein fell into programming at the now-defunct Thalia, a Snob haunt of long standing on New York's Upper West Side, and, since taking the helm of Film Forum's repertory division in 1987, has effectively created several Snob groundswells, such as the vogue for pre–HAYS CODE films wrought by his Before the Code series.

Greenaway, Peter. Arguably the perviest of the Brit-perv director set that includes NICOLAS ROEG,

KEN RUSSELL, and DEREK JARMAN, testing the limits of even the most jaded Arthouse Snobs with his grisly violence, extraordinary pretention, and splotchy-Englishperson frontal nudity. While his early features were merely head-scratchingly opaque—*The Falls* (1980) was an abstract, three-hour mockumentary about an unexplained catastrophe—Greenaway's work quickly became more baroque and nasty, most notably with *The Cook, the Thief, His Wife and Her Lover* (1989), which stars Michael Gambon as a voracious gangster who, after savagely murdering his wife's lover, is forced to eat the fellow's cooked, glazed penis.

GreenCine. Savvy, San Francisco–based DVD-rental company founded in 2002 as a Film Snob's alternative to the intolerably mainstream Netflix. With its hard-to-find titles (e.g., *Bury Me Dead, The Brick Dollhouse*) and requisite perverse and/or obscurist staff recommendations (e.g., Jess Franco's *The Diabolical Doctor Z* and Fassbinder's *Beware of a Holy Whore*), GreenCine affords all the perks of an aggressively hip alterna-store without the unpleasantness of dealing with surly, contemptuous clerks. *I'm stoked! The Criterion* Videodrome *is next up in my* GreenCine *queue!*

Grier, Pam. Tall, regally beautiful black actress who made her name in WIP (women-in-prison) movies in the early seventies before becoming the reigning empress-mama of blaxploitation, kicking and baring ass in such vehicles as *Coffy* (1973; tagline: "She'll cream ya!") and *Foxy Brown* (1974), both of which were written and directed by Jack Hill, a career B-picture director hailed as a genius by Quentin Tarantino for his '75 girl-gang movie *Switchblade Sisters*. After a quiet couple of decades of TV work and supporting roles in movies, Grier was lovingly rehabilitated by Tarantino in his 1997 film *Jackie Brown*, in which she was again a leading lady. Novice Snobs frequently make the mistake of crediting Grier for playing the title character in *Cleopatra Jones* (1973); that role was in fact played by Tamara Dobson.

Pam Grier

Grindhouse. Posthumously coined genre term for the tawdry scuzzploitation films that flourished in sticky-floored adults-only movie houses before the advent of videos and the tidying up of Times Square. Though some film theorists extend grindhouse's reign back to the anti-syphilis scare films of the 1930s (and even lump Tod Browning's *FREAKS* into the category), slumming Snobs associate grindhouse with the late 1960s, early '70s golden era of WIP (women-in-prison) films and the deathless "classics" *I Dismember Mama*, *Gutter Trash*, and *Ilsa, She Wolf of the SS*.

Hall, Conrad. Hard-boiled cinematographer (1926–2003) and son of *Mutiny on the Bounty* author James Norman Hall. As in-demand by rogue American filmmakers as his buddy HASKELL WEXLER in the 1960s and '70s, Hall shot *Cool Hand Luke* (1967), *In Cold Blood* (1967), and *Butch Cassidy and the Sundance Kid* (1969), winning an Oscar for the latter. After a hiatus from cinematography, Hall returned with a vengeance late in his life, winning Oscars for *American Beauty* (1999) and *Road to Perdition* (2002). *At last, the widescreen Fox DVD of* Black Widow *does full justice to Theresa Russell's foxiness and* Conrad Hall*'s neo-noir genius!*

Hammer Films. British production company that, in its factory-like production of blood-soaked, décolletage-heavy horror flicks from the 1950s to the '70s, was an overseas cousin to the United States's AIP, only with a better roster of actors. The Albionically gaunt Christopher Lee and Peter Cushing became famous for playing endless iterations of, respectively, Dracula and Dr. Frankenstein (eliciting the admiration of Francis Ford Coppola, Martin Scorsese, and, especially, George Lucas, who cast both men in *Star Wars* films), while Oliver Reed hammed it up as a werewolf, and Bette Davis, in the throes of her run as a ROBERT ALDRICH horror hag, starred as the title character of *The Nanny*, in which she got to drown a child in a bathtub.

Harris, Robert A., and James C. Katz. Affable, chrome-domed film restorers who, since the 1980s, have toiled nobly to preserve America's film heritage, most celebratedly on their reconstruction of David Lean's *Lawrence of Arabia* (1962), which was originally released in 70mm widescreen format at 222 minutes, later cut to 187 minutes, and eventually left to molder in storage, until Harris and Katz recovered missing footage, and, to rapturous response in 1989, premiered their 218-minute version. Specializing in large-format 1950s and '60s fare—*Spartacus, My Fair Lady, Vertigo, Rear Window*—Harris and Katz evangelize about the crappy state of film preservation even today, noting that many so-called "restorations" for theatrical and DVD rerelease are simply patch jobs, and not painstaking restorations of films from their original negatives. *Damn, I wish* The Magnificent Ambersons *could get the* Harris-and-Katz *treatment!*

Harryhausen, Ray. Animator and visual-effects maestro (born in 1920) behind a series of terrifying films, putatively for children, that combined stop-motion animation with live action. In such films as *Jason and the Argonauts* (1963), *The Golden Voyage of Sinbad* (1974), and *Sinbad and the Eye of the Tiger* (1977), spray-tanned actors and actresses did furious battle with stiffly moving but nevertheless nightmare-inducing centaurs, minotaurs, walking statues, and other exotic predators. Though his filmography is more familiar to Kitsch Snobs than to kids, Harryhausen was awarded an honorary Oscar for his work in 1992, and was slyly namechecked in the Pixar film *Monsters, Inc.* (2001).

Hawks, Howard. Prolific, genre-hopping American director (1896–1977) retroactively assigned visionary status by French and American proponents of the AUTEUR THEORY. Technically proficient and overflowing with ideas (such as having Cary Grant and Rosalind Russell accelerate the pace of their speech in *His Girl Friday* to suit the movie's frenetic newsroom setting), Hawks proved adept at noir (*The Big Sleep*), screwball comedy (*Bringing Up Baby, Ball of Fire*), and widescreen Westerns (*Red River, Rio Lobo*), but his films bore no authorial trademark. Nevertheless, French worship of his films, which Hawks often produced himself, proved crucial in shaping the cult of the director-as-godhead.

Hays Code. Nickname for the "family values"–upholding Motion Picture Production Code, which was drafted in 1930 by Will H. Hays, an ex–Republican National Committee chairman enlisted by the movie industry to head its Motion Picture Producers and Distributors of America (MPPDA) organization. Implemented in 1934, at a time when early Hollywood's moguls were taking flak for the moral bankruptcy of their product, the Hays Code forbade the making of any film that "will lower the moral standards of those who see it," as well as any depictions of "illegal drug trafficking," "miscegenation," "lustful embraces," flag desecration, and the like. What the jug-eared Hays (whom Gore Vidal likened physically to Mickey Mouse) didn't know was that he was effectively creating two Snob cults, one for the licentious pre-code talkies of the early 1930s (such as *Baby Face*, in which Barbara Stanwyck plays a sexually voracious bar wench who sleeps her way to the top of a banking company, and the gangster films *Public Enemy* and *Scarface*), and another for the layers of entendre and innuendo that writers and directors came up with in the 1940s and '50s to outsmart the code (e.g., Lauren Bacall's famous line to Humphrey Bogart in *To Have and Have Not*, "You know how to whistle, don't you, Steve? You just put your lips together—and *blow*"). The Hays Code was enforced until the late sixties, when it was superseded by the modern ratings code that warns viewers against potentially naughty content.

Hellman, Monte. Hitless cult director, among ROGER CORMAN's many protégés, who found his muse in scraggly character actor Warren Oates and remains best known for three of his earlier films: the "existential" (read: slow) Western *The Shooting* (1967), in which Oates starred with Jack Nicholson; the meandering (read: slow) road movie *Two-Lane Blacktop* (1971), in which Oates starred with James Taylor and the Beach Boys' Dennis Wilson; and the offbeat (read: slow) drama *Cockfighter* (1974), in which Oates costarred with some roosters and didn't actually speak until the final scene.

Herrmann, Bernard. Film-music composer extraordinaire (1911–75) who did more to contribute to the mood of the movies he worked on than any of his peers, most notably with the infamous, sawing *Wheeek! Wheeek! Wheeek!* strings during *Psycho*'s shower sequence. A colleague of Orson Welles's since the prodigy director's radio days with the Mercury Theatre, Herrmann went on to score *Citizen Kane* (1941) and *The Magnificent Ambersons*

(1942) before getting scooped up by Alfred Hitchcock, appropriated from Hitchcock by François Truffaut, and enjoying an edifying late career as a favorite of MOVIENESS-obsessed young auteurs such as Brian De Palma (*Sisters*, 1973) and Martin Scorsese (*Taxi Driver*, 1976, Herrmann's last commission). Even posthumously, Herrmann has remained in demand, with his original, 1962 soundtrack for *Cape Fear* faithfully re-created for Scorsese's '91 remake, his *Vertigo* music used for Terry Gilliam's *Twelve Monkeys* (1995), his circa-1968 *Twisted Nerve* music appropriated by Quentin Tarantino for *Kill Bill: Vol. 1* (2003), and his *Psycho* music used for comic effect every time some young, Jason Biggs–like nebbish actor feels "stalked" by an improbably beautiful woman.

Bernard Herrmann

Hixploitation. Curious seventies-SPLOITATION sub-genre in which Hollywood devoted an inordinate amount of attention to the redneck, yee-haw South, resulting in a spate of films about car chases, vigilante justice, road trips, and backwoods terror. Tracing its roots to John Boorman's hillbilly-hell opus *Deliverance* (1972) and the vengeance-in-Tennessee tale *Walking Tall* (1973), hixploitation blossomed with *The Klansman* (1974), in which Alabama sheriff Lee Marvin presided over residents O.J. Simpson and Richard Burton; Jonathan Demme's *Citizens Band* (1977); SAM PECKINPAH's timely capitalization on the CB and truckin' crazes, *Convoy* (1978), in which Kris Kristofferson's trucker outsmarted Ernest

Borgnine's fat cop; and Clint Eastwood's massively successful orangutan movies, *Every Which Way But Loose* (1978) and *Any Which Way You Can* (1980). The apotheosis of the hixploitation movement was *Smokey and the Bandit* (1977), the directorial debut of Tennessee-born veteran stuntman Hal Needham, who actually cast Mel Tillis, Foster Brooks, and Ruth Buzzi for unironic effect.

Hopper, Dennis. Survivor-actor who, like ROBERT EVANS, has parlayed his rough, California-dream-gone-sour voyage through the darkness into lovable-nut status and near-universal adoration. Appearing on the scene in the 1950s, where he was a friend and castmate of James Dean's, Hopper earned a reputation as a "difficult" actor, his stubbornness redeemed only when the small-budget druggie film he directed, cowrote, and costarred in, *Easy Rider* (1969), became a hit and generational touchstone. But Hopper never quite capitalized on this triumph, Hoovering cocaine and living for a time in Mexico (and resurfacing just long enough to "play" a raving loon in *Apocalypse Now*). By the 1980s, however, a cleaned-up, gray-templed Hopper won good notices in *Blue Velvet* and *Hoosiers,* opening the door for a lucrative latter-day life as a supervillain (*Speed*) and modern-art collector. If pressed, Snobs will argue that Hopper's best work is as the director of two films nobody has seen, *The Last Movie* (1971) and *Out of the Blue* (1980).

Howard, Clint. Cult actor with squeaky voice and enormous cranium, best known for his brief appearances in the

movies of A-list older brother Ron, though more regularly employed in TV shows and B pictures, often as a *Deliverance*-esque hillbilly threat. Like Ron, Clint acted as a child, notoriously starring, at age seven, in one of the oddest *Star Trek* episodes ever, "The Corbomite Maneuver," in which he played a babylike alien, mouthing words spoken by an adult actor.

Clint Howard

I Am Curious—Yellow. Ponderous, nudity-filled 1967 Swedish film, directed by Vilgot Sjöman, that sparked a moralists-versus-libertines kerfuffle upon its American release in 1969, with prints of it being seized at U.S. Customs and Norman Mailer championing the film, with characteristic hyperbole, as "one of the most important pictures that I have ever seen in my life." A very of-its-time film about a young woman's sexual and political "voyage of discovery," with explicit sex scenes between its lumpy-bodied leads, Lena Nyman and Börje Ahlstedt, and pseudo-documentary interludes about Martin Luther King and Soviet poet Yevgeny Yevtushenko, *I Am Curious—Yellow* effectively nailed the coffin shut on the HAYS CODE and paved the way for routine female nudity in mainstream features (though male nudity would become primarily the province of KEN RUSSELL and the Merchant-Ivory team). Long out of print, its title better known than its content, *I Am Curious—Yellow* has belatedly received the CRITERION COLLECTION treatment, coming neatly packaged in a box set with Sjöman's follow-up, *I Am Curious—Blue.*

Iranian New Wave. The most heavily Snob-championed foreign-film movement of the early twenty-first century, posited by such crit-worthies as JONATHAN ROSEN-BAUM as being as important as the FRENCH NEW WAVE of the 1950s and '60s. Though the origins of the Iranian New Wave date back to the late sixties, when Dariush Mehrjui's naturalist film *The Cow* attracted international attention—alerting both Iranians and outsiders to the possibility of a smarter alternative to Filmfarsi, the nation's BOLLYWOOD-like brand of indigenous cineschlock—the New Wave truly gained traction in the late nineties, when Mohsen Makhmalbaf's *Gabbeh* won limited American release and Abbas Kiarostami's *Taste of Cherry* shared the Palme d'Or with a Japanese film at the 1997 Cannes Film Festival. Ever since, Makhmalbaf and Kiarostami's films (such as the former's timely, Taliban-tastic 2001 movie, *Kandahar*) have become major Snob causes célèbres with props kicked to them by, among others, Jean-Luc Godard. Makhmalbaf has even begat his own, Coppola-like extended family of New Wavers, with his wife, Marzieh Meshkini, his daughter, Samira Makhmalbaf, and his most famous leading man, Majid Majidi, all becoming filmmakers. *Samira Makhmalbaf's astonishing debut,* The Apple, *portends a bright future for the* Iranian New Wave, *and was well worth the two-hour drive through the snow to the Facets Cinémathèque.*

Italian neorealism. A movement that emerged at the tail end of World War II that was characterized by realistic portrayals of the lives of the lower classes and the use of nonactors and authentic locations. Though its touchstone texts, Vittorio De Sica's *The Bicycle Thief* and Roberto Rossellini's *Open City*, are moving, their spareness makes them tough going to sit through, and the movement was quickly eclipsed, in the estimates of Snobs and ordinary Italians, by the emergence of CINECITTÀ-style extravagance and decadence.

Jackson, Peter. New Zealand–born director whose stewardship of the *Lord of the Rings* trilogy has eclipsed his true Snob credentials as the gonzo creator-director of *Bad Taste* (1987), his micro-budget splatter-comedy debut, which unexpectedly made a splash at Cannes, and its two follow-ups, *Meet the Feebles* (a 1989 satire of show business enacted entirely by filthy-talking, drug-taking puppets) and *Braindead* (an ultraviolent 1992 zombie flick, released in America as *Dead Alive*).

Jaglom, Henry. Rumpledly handsome, staggeringly self-indulgent filmmaker whose chattery, mostly improvised comedies, such as *Always* (1985), *Eating* (1990), and *Festival in Cannes* (2002), bear the imprimaturs of both 1970s psychotherapy and 1950s coffeehouse philosophizing (as such, earning Jaglom not quite fully accurate comparisons to Woody Allen and JOHN CASSAVETES). Though his films are seldom shown outside art houses, what truly endears Jaglom to Snobs is his role as Orson Welles's post–PETER BOGDANOVICH caretaker; Jaglom kept the great man company in his last years and gave Welles his final role in the younger director's

THE TEN GREAT UBIQUITOUS OVERWEIGHT VETERAN CHARACTER ACTORS OF THE MODERN CINEMATIC ERA

A Spotter's Guide for Film Snobs

Joe Don Baker

Seen in such films as: *Walking Tall* (1973); *Charley Varrick* (1973); *Fletch* (1985); *Cape Fear* (1991)

Characterly characteristics: Squinty-eyed, southern, volatile

Auteur sponsor(s): Don Siegel, Martin Scorsese

Martin Balsam

Seen in such films as: *12 Angry Men* (1957); *Psycho* (1960); *The Taking of Pelham One Two Three* (1974); *Murder on the Orient Express* (1974)

Characterly characteristics: Haggard, sad-sack, cranky
Auteur sponsor(s): Sidney Lumet

Wilford Brimley

Seen in such films as: *The Electric Horseman*
(1979); *Absence of Malice* (1981); *The Natural*
(1984); *Cocoon* (1985); *The Firm* (1993)
Characterly characteristics: Grandfatherly, extrav-
agantly mustachioed, cornpone
Auteur sponsor(s): Sydney Pollack, Robert Redford

Brian Dennehy

Seen in such films as: *Foul Play* (1978); *Cocoon*
(1985); *Silverado* (1985); *F/X* (1986); *Presumed
Innocent* (1990)
Characterly characteristics: Stocky, volatile, Irish-
American
Auteur sponsor(s): Alan J. Pakula

Charles Durning

Seen in such films as: *Sisters* (1973); *The Muppet
Movie* (1979); *Tootsie* (1982); *The Hudsucker
Proxy* (1994); *O Brother, Where Are Thou* (2000)
Characterly characteristics: Jowly, buffoonish,
southern-ish, cornpone

Auteur sponsor(s): Brian De Palma, the Coen brothers

Lou Jacobi

Seen in such films as: *Everything You Always Wanted to Know About Sex (But Were Afraid to Ask)* (1972); *Next Stop, Greenwich Village* (1976); *My Favorite Year* (1982); *Avalon* (1990)

Characterly characteristics: Jowly, grandfatherly, mustachioed, cranky, Jewish

Auteur sponsor(s): Barry Levinson, Paul Mazursky, Woody Allen

Kenneth McMillan

Seen in such films as: *The Taking of Pelham One Two Three* (1974); *Ragtime* (1981); *Amadeus* (1984), *Runaway Train* (1985)

Characterly characteristics: Broad-faced, ruddy, buffoonish

Auteur sponsor(s): Milos Forman

Fred Dalton Thompson

Seen in such films as: *No Way Out* (1987); *The Hunt for Red October* (1990); *Cape Fear* (1991); *In the Line of Fire* (1993)

Characterly characteristics: Jowly, senatorial, south-
ern, cornpone
Auteur sponsor(s): Roger Donaldson, TV auteur
Dick Wolf (*Law & Order*)

M. Emmet Walsh

Seen in such films as: *What's Up, Doc* (1972); *Slap
Shot* (1977); *Blade Runner* (1982); *Blood Simple*
(1984)
Characterly characteristics: Jowly, southern-ish,
cranky
Auteur sponsor(s): Peter Bogdanovich, the Coen
brothers

Jack Warden

Seen in such films as: *12 Angry Men* (1957); *Bye Bye
Braverman* (1968); *Heaven Can Wait* (1978);
. . . And Justice for All (1979); *Being There* (1979);
Bullets Over Broadway (1994)
Characterly characteristics: Jowly, presidential,
cranky
Auteur sponsor(s): Hal Ashby, Sidney Lumet,
Warren Beatty, Woody Allen

Someone to Love (1987), in which Welles simply sat in the back of a theater and spoke his mind with characteristic orotundity.

Jarman, Derek. Audaciously decadent and self-indulgent Brit-perv director (1942–94) who, in the loucheness stakes, one-upped even mentor KEN RUSSELL, with whom Jarman got his start designing sets in the seventies. Jarman's films are characterized by stunning visual tableaus, goofy, deliberate anachronisms, and incoherence: *Sebastiane* (1976) has all-Latin dialogue; *Caravaggio* (1986) puts the sixteenth-century painter and his gay lover on motorcycles; the fourteenth-century drama *Edward II* (1992) features a sudden appearance by Annie Lennox singing Cole Porter; *Wittgenstein* (1993) engages the philosopher in debates with a little green Martian. Jarman's final film, *Blue*, consists of the titular color projected uninterruptedly for 75 minutes while portions of the director's diary, written while he was dying of AIDS, are played on the soundtrack.

Kael, Pauline. Revered film critic (1919–2001) whose work, most of which appeared in *The New Yorker*, stood out for its bracing, provocative prose and its author's loony, nonsensical taste; no one was smarter and more cogent about Cary Grant's career and Steven Spielberg's early films, yet no one was more reckless in overpraising grim 1970s murk and unbearably blowsy female performances (e.g., Elizabeth Taylor in *X Y & Zee*; Karen Black in *Come Back to the 5 & Dime*,

Jimmy Dean, Jimmy Dean; Bette Midler in *Big Business*).
A tiny woman, Kael nevertheless inspired
fear in her legions of movie-critic acolytes
(known as "Paulettes"), full-grown men
and women who tremulously sought
her unforthcoming approval and pil-
grimaged to her home in the Berkshires
in the vain hope of being anointed her
heir apparent.

Pauline Kael

Katz, Ephraim. Industrious Israeli-born film nerd
who, in the 1970s, single-handedly undertook the task
of compiling an encylopedia of film. Published in
1979, after years of work, Katz's *The Film Encyclopedia*
quickly established itself as the definitive film reference
for both Snobs who need to know what a "friction
head" is (it's a kind of tripod head that ensures smooth
camera movement) and laypersons who can't keep
Linda Darnell straight from Joan Blondell. Katz died in
1992, and successive, expanded editions of the *Film
Encyclopedia* have been produced by his protégés,
though hard-core Snobs take issue with some of the
cuts that were made from Katz's original, and keep the
'79 edition around.

Kauffmann, Stanley. Super-tenured *New Republic* film
critic (born in 1916, with the magazine since 1958)
who helped foment art-house enthusiasm for foreign
films in the 1960s—he adores ITALIAN NEOREAL-
ISM, Federico Fellini, Akira Kurosawa, and Satyajit

Ray—but strenuously disagreed with PAULINE KAEL and her ilk about the merits of the French New Wave and the *EASY RIDERS, RAGING BULLS*-generation filmmakers, deeming them overrated. An unblurbable iconoclast in a Peter Travers age, Kauffmann perseveres in a time-warped intellectualist cocoon, conveying carnal excitement only when his crush, Emma Thompson, appears in a film.

Kehr, Dave. Third- or possibly even fourth-string *New York Times* movie critic. Though often relegated to reviewing DVD releases, he is preferred by Snobs over A. O. Scott, Manohla Dargis, and Stephen Holden.

Kuchar brothers. Twin filmmakers (Mike and George, born in 1942 of Bronx-tenement pedigree) whose low-budget, high-camp films predated John Waters's and were more naïfish and insouciant than those of their contemporaries Andy Warhol and Kenneth Anger, making them the semi-unwitting darlings of the sixties New York underground. The brothers are still active today, though more on solo projects than joint ones. *I can't decide if I should go to the* Kuchar brothers *retrospective or the Lisa Cholodenko double feature at the Queer Arts Festival.*

Langdon, Harry. Baby-faced star of 1920s TWO-REELERS who briefly ranked among the comic greats (alongside Charlie Chaplin, Harold Lloyd, and Buster Keaton) but died in 1944, semi-forgotten and in reduced circumstances, thereby setting himself up to be posthumously rehabilitated by JAMES AGEE, and, later, by toking proto-Snob college students during the silent-comedy revival of the 1960s. Langdon earns further Snob points for having been Frank Capra's conduit to the big time, starring in Capra's first two features, *The Strong Man* (1926) and *Long Pants* (1927), before getting a swelled head, dismissing Capra as his collaborator, and proceeding to flounder as his own writer-director.

Harry Langdon

Laser disc. Outmoded digital-video format, introduced in the early 1980s but superseded by the DVD in the late '90s. Though the unwieldy, pizza-size disc never caught on in the mass market, Snob purists insist that it offers superior picture and sound quality, and pride themselves on owning out-of-print, special-feature-enhanced discs from the CRITERION COLLECTION. *Dude, I just found a* laser disc *of* Blade Runner *on eBay!*

L'Atalante. Sumptuously shot but soul-crushingly dull 1934 French film that takes place aboard a barge floating down the Seine. While the film's surrealist touches and claustrophobic love story endear it to Snobs, *L'Atalante* owes much of its cult status to a familiar mystique-building postproduction narrative—it was "butchered" by its producers and finally restored to its rightful length in 1989—and to the fact that its star-crossed young director, Jean Vigo, died of leukemia the year of the movie's release.

Laughlin, Tom. Eccentric writer-director-producer-star of the 1971 movie *Billy Jack*, a queasy melding of hippie proselytizing, proto–CHOP-SOCKY fight sequences, and Costnerish embrace of Native American wisdom. Filmed on a tiny budget outside of the studio system, *Billy Jack* is a Snob rallying point, though it resides in an uncertain place between kitsch classic and fearless feat of maverick seventies filmmaking. Laughlin tends carefully to his cult, selling tapes of his lectures on Jungian psychology and occasionally threatening to run for president and/or make more films.

Léaud, Jean-Pierre. Fidgety, chain-smoking actor who at age fifteen landed, literally, the role of his lifetime, as the wayward adolescent Antoine Doinel in François Truffaut's *The 400 Blows* (1959). Throughout the sixties and seventies, Léaud remained the face of the FRENCH NEW WAVE, playing Doinel in three more Truffaut features and appearing in several iconic films by Jean-Luc Godard, as well as starring in Jean Eustache's sexual-revolution epic *The Mother and the Whore* (1973) and offering much-needed comic relief in Bernardo Bertolucci's *Last Tango in Paris* (1972). More recently he has become, like SEYMOUR CASSELL, an homage-object for various artiste directors, playing a washed-up filmmaker in Olivier Assayas's *Irma Vep* (1996) and himself in both

Ming-liang Tsai's *What Time Is It There?* (2001) and Bertolucci's *The Dreamers* (2003).

Letterbox. DVD and VHS format that allows home-video viewers who don't own widescreen TVs to watch movies in close approximation of their original ASPECT RATIO; so named for the horizontal, mail-slot-like band of screen that appears between two black bars when a 16:9-source film is adapted to fit the 4:3 screen of a TV without losing the whole picture. *Watching the 4:3 version of* Return of the Jedi *is not only idiotic, given that Lucasfilm offers it in* letterbox, *it's an affront to all the work Lucas put into those reissues!*

Lewis, Herschell Gordon. Dilettante filmmaker hailed by Snobs as the Godfather of Splatter. On a lark, Lewis, who to this day works full-time as an advertising executive, began making low-budget, excessively gory movies in the early sixties, among them *Blood Feast, Two Thousand Maniacs!,* and *The Gruesome Twosome*—all required titles for anyone wishing to flaunt trash credentials.

Luddy, Tom. Extremely socially active film archivist, producer, and festival organizer, based in Berkeley, California. Having run the Pacific Film Archive, worked at Francis Ford Coppola's American Zoetrope, and produced such off-center eighties films as *Barfly* and PAUL SCHRADER's *Mishima,* Luddy is known for being awe-

Tom Luddy

somely well connected in the art-house world, and for facilitating connections among film people, art people, critics, and leftist culturati the world over. *I was introduced to Fassbinder by* Tom Luddy *at a party at Francis's.*

Lupino, Ida. Actress-director valued by Snobs not for her string of tough-gal roles in the 1940s, but for directing the pulpy '50s dramas *Outrage, Hard, Fast and Beautiful,* and *The Hitch-Hiker,* and for playing the sadistic warden in *Women's Prison,* the ur-text of the WIP (women-in-prison) genre. A rare female godhead for the generally estrophobic Snob community.

MacGuffin. Whimsical term for a seemingly crucial but actually trivial plot element—such as the bottled uranium in Alfred Hitchcock's *Notorious,* or the stolen $40,000 in his *Psycho*—that sets a thriller's frenzied action in motion. Coined by the screenwriter Angus MacPhail, who wrote *Spellbound* for Hitchcock and nonsensically defined a MacGuffin as "a device for killing lions in the Scottish Highlands" (where there are no lions), the term has transcended the Film Snob world to become a rhetorical trope for middle-aged Op-Ed columnists.

Maddin, Guy. Winnipeg-born director, often referred to in priggish film-crit circles as a "fabulist," whose genuinely strange movies combine a GERMAN EXPRESSIONISM–informed visual sense with an arch sense of humor and a Farrelly Brothers–like fetish for disabled and deranged persons. Achieving cult status with his first full-length feature, *Tales from the Gimli Hospital* (1988), the rollicking story of two smallpox-quarantined lunkheads, filmed in black and white, Maddin fully arrived as the new baron of the Art Snob set with *The Saddest Music in the World* (2004), which starred Isabella Rossellini as a perturbed, legless beer baroness. The director's column in *FILM COMMENT*, "My Jolly Corner," in which he breezily celebrates such obscurities as NICHOLAS RAY's *The Lusty Men*, is the best thing in that otherwise mirthless magazine.

Malick, Terrence. Salingeresquely private Texas writer-director who, shrewdly or unwittingly, has cultivated American filmdom's greatest mystique by shunning publicity and very infrequently making films. After a relatively prolific 1970s in which he made two lyrical, impressionistic pictures at odds with the propulsive grit of his *EASY RIDERS, RAGING BULLS*–era contemporaries—*Badlands* (1973), loosely based on Charles Starkweather's fifties murdering spree, and *Days of Heaven* (1978), set in Texas and beautifully shot by NÉSTOR ALMENDROS—Malick disappeared for two decades, finally returning with an adaptation of James Jones's World War II novel *The Thin Red Line* that, characteristically, was hard to follow and lovely to look at. On a creative jag of sorts, Malick has pressed on in the twenty-first century with two epic projects, *The New World*, based on the John Smith–Pochahontas legend, and a biopic of Che Guevara.

"IT GETS BETTER WITH REPEATED VIEWINGS!"

Keeping the Good Snob Stuff Straight from the Crap

Though Film Snobs pride themselves on their precisely calibrated taste, they are also perverse creatures, lavishing praise on flagrant hack-work whose creators didn't give a damn. ("That's what makes it so *brilliant,* so *audacious!*") Or, sometimes, Snobs will actually delude themselves, persuading themselves that the cinematic mulch to which they have devoted countless hours and self-financed Web 'zines must have some significant, doctoral-dissertation-worthy cultural import that the small-minded, Tom Cruise–adoring public doesn't grasp. Herewith, a consumer's guide to Snob trustworthiness.

Ten Worthwhile Snob Causes Célèbres

Robert Aldrich
John Cassavetes
Manny Farber
Freaks
French New Wave
German Expressionism
Guy Maddin
Sam Peckinpah
Spaghetti Westerns
Wire-fu

Ten Fraudulent Snob Causes Célèbres

Ai No Corrida
Maya Deren
Dogme 95
Robert Downey Sr.
Peter Greenaway
L'Atalante
Tom Laughlin
Mexican wrestling pictures
Office Space
WIP (women-in-prison) flicks

Maltin, Leonard. Bearded, bespectacled movie critic whose adenoidal speaking voice and poindexterish appearance as *Entertainment Tonight*'s movie critic belie the fact that he commands a fair amount of respect among Film Snobs, mostly for his indispensable, annually published *Leonard Maltin's Movie Guide*, a *Zagat's*-like reference book that encapsulates virtually every film available on video. Snobs refer to the guide, anthropomorphically, as "Maltin." *Jesus, I can't believe I forgot the year* Greed *came out! Better look it up in* Maltin.

Leonard Maltin

Mankiewicz, Herman. Gruff, whiskey-soaked, cigar-chomping old-school screenwriter par excellence (1897–1953) who bolted his comfy perch at the Algonquin Roundtable to write titles for silent films and screenplays for talkies, famously summoning his friend Ben Hecht west with the line "Millions are to be grabbed out here and your only competition is idiots." A dab hand at many genres—he wrote or cowrote *Dinner at Eight*, the Marx Brothers' *Duck Soup*, and *The Pride of the Yankees*—Mankiewicz posthumously became the center of an enormous Snob controversy when PAULINE KAEL, in a two-part 1971 *New Yorker* article entitled "Raising Kane," argued somewhat nonsensically that Mankiewicz, more than Orson Welles, was the driving creative force behind *Citizen Kane*. Though such Welles acolytes as PETER BOGDANOVICH handily shot down this claim, Kael succeeded in burnishing the legend of "Mank," who, in time-honored old-Hollywood fashion, had died unloved and penniless.

Mankiewicz, Joseph L. Urbane writer-director (1909–93) and younger brother of HERMAN MANKIEWICZ who remains the only person to win double Oscars (for best director and best screenplay) in consecutive years, for *A Letter to Three Wives* (1949) and *All About Eve* (1950). Though Technique Snobs are wont to lay into Mankiewicz for his stagy shots and lack of Wellesian flourish, Screenplay Snobs adore him for his literate, Anglophilically cynical dialogue. (His films often include a snide English dispenser of bons mots, usually Rex Harrison or George Sanders.) Nearly undone mentally and physically by the salvage job he was called in to perform on the tabloid armageddon that was the Elizabeth Taylor–Richard Burton *Cleopatra* (1963), Mankiewicz recovered sufficiently to become one of Hollywood's most entertaining old cranks.

Maysles brothers, the. Unnervingly nonjudgmental twin-brother documentarians (Albert and David, born in 1926; David died in 1987), known for their voyeuristic, deadpan depictions of milieus scary (the chaotic, deadly Rolling Stones concert at the Altamont Speedway in 1970's *Gimme Shelter*), disturbing (the gone-to-seed Hamptons mansion of mentally ill Jackie O. cousins "Big Edie" and "Little Edie" Beale in 1976's *Grey Gardens*), and pathetic (the drab, Lomanish world of door-to-door Bible salesmen in 1969's *Salesman*).

Since David's death, Albert has soldiered on as cinema verité's éminence grise, making new films and attending lovingly to the CRITERION COLLECTION reissues of their 1960s and '70s work.

McKee, Robert. Theatrically belligerent, fiercely browed screenwriting guru whose revival-like three-day Story Seminars attract thousands of desperate would-be auteurs, a zillionth of whom actually become successful in pictures. At once a bracing, incisive instructor and a willfully demoralizing lowerer of expectations (for both his students' prospects and the future of film), McKee, who has been on the circuit since the 1980s, has digested many of his lessons into his 1997 book, *Story* (an essential Snob text), and consented to have the actor Brian Cox portray him fairly accurately in the Spike Jonze–Charlie Kaufman film *Adaptation* (2002).

Robert McKee

Meditation on. Stock hack-crit phrase used to bestow an air of erudition and gravitas on both the critic and the film he is reviewing. *Sofia Coppola's* Lost in Translation *is an affecting* meditation on *cultural and temporal dislocation; the* Matrix *series is the Wachowski brothers'* meditation on *the intersection of technology and spirituality.*

Mekas, Jonas. Lithuanian-born, New York–based overlord of avant-garde film. Born in 1922, Mekas, a World War II refugee, founded *Film*

Culture in his new homeland in 1954 as a sort of American answer to *CAHIERS DU CINÉMA*, and cemented his Snob martyrdom a decade later by getting arrested for screening Jack Smith's *FLAMING CREATURES*. In 1970, Mekas founded Anthology Film Archives, to this day New York's foremost temple for pallid worshippers of STAN BRAKHAGE and MAYA DEREN, and in 2001, Mekas's own career as an underground filmmaker reached its apogee with the nearly five-hour-long *As I Was Moving Ahead Occasionally I Saw Brief Glimpses of Beauty*, essentially a shapeless compendium of thirty years' worth of home movies.

Mexican wrestling pictures. Bizarre trash genre of the 1960s in which masked Mexican wrestlers—the most popular of whom was called El Santo—did battle with zombies, robots, mummies, and evil scientists in schlock-horror films whose rock-bottom production values made Ed Wood look like James Cameron. The U.S. versions, horrifically dubbed and translated (and in which El Santo was called Samson), were even worse and have come to be fetishized by aficionados, one of whom publishes a 'zine, *Santo Street*, devoted to the genre. *My wife's mad at me; I passed out on the couch watching* Mexican wrestling pictures *on the USA Network again.*

Miike, Takashi. Wildly prolific Japanese director whose unhinged, ultraviolent action films, such as *Dead or Alive* (2000) and *Ichi the Killer* (2001), have established him as the godhead of Asiaphile Splatter Snobs. Even so,

Miike's willfully weird oeuvre eludes strict "horror" classification: *Audition* (1999), about a middle-aged widower seeking a new wife, shifts abruptly from Meg Ryan–ish romantic comedy to an epic torture sequence (including acupuncture-needle abuse and an amputation by steel wire) that sent American moviegoers out of art houses literally retching, while *Happiness of the Katakuris* (2001), about a mountain inn plagued by zombies, includes some MGM-style musical production numbers.

Milius, John. Hyperbolically martial screenwriter-director and iconoclastic Hollywood far-righty; the most raging and bullish member of the Scorsese-Coppola-Spielberg-etc. generation. Deemed unfit for military service in Vietnam on account of his asthma, Milius channeled his virility and bloodlust into writing or cowriting the first two *Dirty Harry* movies, *Apocalypse Now, Conan the Barbarian*, and *Red Dawn*, the latter two of which he also directed. Per Snob lore, Milius was the inspiration for John Goodman's 'Nam-obsessed character in the Coen brothers' *The Big Lebowski*.

Mini-DV. Abbreviation for "miniature digital video," the preferred format of both independent filmmakers shooting on a shoestring and affluent directors seeking to infuse their films with a frisson of guerrilla intransigence. Steven Soderbergh used Canon's XL1S Mini-DV camera to shoot *Full Frontal*, his DOGME 95 homage. *For my next*

Mini-DV

film, everyone's working for free, and we're shooting it entirely on Mini-DV *in Casey Affleck's garage.*

Mise-en-scène. Theorist-beloved term describing the collective elements of a scene, from sets, costumes, and lighting to the positioning of the characters; best uttered while gesticulating with a lit cigarette between index and middle fingers. *With the painstaking single-shot* mise-en-scène *of* Russian Ark, *Sokurov self-consciously distances himself from Eisenstein.*

Mitchell, Cameron. Ursine veteran character actor (1918–94) with an astonishingly long list of horror and straight-to-video credits; the Brian Dennehy of the B's. Though he had "straight" roles in the 1950s studio films *How to Marry a Millionaire* and *Carousel,* Mitchell derived his Snob cred from playing military men and police officers in such obscure eighties splatter pix as *Rage to Kill, Killpoint,* and *Kill Squad.*

Mondo Cane. Nominal documentary that prefigured the Fox Network–style "shockumentary" by some decades. Made in 1962 by two Italian filmmakers, *Mondo Cane* became a midnight-movie staple by placing pseudo-serious commentary over disturbing pseudo-anthropological footage of rich and poor societies (e.g., grotesque California housewives burying their dogs at a pet cemetery, Chinese eating dogs) and scenes of *National Geographic*–style frontal nudity. In the pre-video age, the word *mondo* (which means, simply, "world") came to signify cinematic transgression, as evidenced by the rash of crapola imitators (*Mondo Bizarro, Mondo Teeno*, etc.) it inspired.

Monograph. A treatise on a particular subject; in film-studies terms, an appreciative study of a particular director's work, often published in conjunction with a museum or university retrospective. Getting assigned to write a monograph is often a young film-school nerd's entrée into the greater Film Snob world. *After I wrote the monograph on Andrei Tarkovsky for L'Institut du Cinéma Difficile, some cultural officials from Belgrade asked me to curate their film festival.*

Morricone, Ennio. Prolific Italian soundtrack composer, most notable for his work on his old schoolmate Sergio Leone's famous SPAGHETTI WESTERNS *A Fistful of Dollars; The Good, the Bad and the Ugly;* and *Once Upon a Time in the West.* Though Morricone continues to churn out scores for both Hollywood and European movies, it's his atmospheric 1960s work that has made him the patron saint of both Soundtrack Snobs and the people who program the iPods in high-end women's-clothing boutiques.

MOS. In-joke filmmaking term, written on a slate or in a screenplay to denote a scene filmed without audio. The etymology is a subject of hot debate, some saying the abbreviation stands for "mute on sound" or "mike offstage," but most taking the prevailing Snob line that the term originated with such transplanted Austrian directors as Erich von Stroheim and Josef von Sternberg, who would call for scenes to be shot "mit out sound."

Movieness. Stock hack-crit term used, like a more fun version of *postmodern*, to denote a director's or viewer's hyperawareness of filmic conventions and techniques. *Watching* Kill Bill*'s gory, kinetic fight scenes, you can sense Tarantino exulting in the sheer* movieness *of moviemaking.*

Mr. Ned. Manhattan tailor shop that became an unlikely Snob destination when word got out that it is where director Wes Anderson gets his too-short, too-narrow prepster suits made. Young obsessives with means and sufficient leanness (hardly a given in Snob circles) are known to seek out Vahram Mateosian, Anderson's tailor, for the latest in moleskin and velvet Wes-wear.

Murch, Walter. Exacting, innovative sound designer who was cultivated by Francis Ford Coppola and George Lucas early in their careers; for Snobs, the genius of film sound. An eccentric, intelligent polymath, Murch dabbles in the other aspects of filmmaking—he cowrote the screenplay to Lucas's *THX 1138* and edited *The English Patient* and *Cold Mountain*—as well as beekeeping. *I'm not easily impressed, but* Murch's *work on the opening sequence of* Apocalypse Now *was next-level shit.*

Negulesco, Jean. Romanian-born director (1900–93) who parlayed his beginnings as a painter in 1920s Paris and set designer in 1930s Hollywood into a glorious mid-career run in the 1950s as a director of high-gloss, pastel-colored films for 20th Century-Fox, including *How to Marry a Millionaire* (1953), *Woman's World* (1954), and *The Best of Everything* (1959)—all of which concern the trials and tribulations of being a begloved, bosomy New York City lady trying to balance the demands of men, the workplace, and heavily under-wired brassieres. Though often compared to DOUG-LAS SIRK, Negulesco kept things frothier and held the high melodrama in check, even as he presided over one of the seminal moments in Kitsch Snob history, in which an office gal–aspiring actress played by fifties supermodel Suzy Parker goes insane after being spurned by her director paramour (played by Pepé Le Pew–like Continental loverman Louis Jourdan).

Nykvist, Sven. Swedish cinematographer who, by virtue of his early renown as Ingmar Bergman's regular camera-man and his later work for Woody Allen, Philip Kaufman, and ANDREI TARKOVSKY, among others, has earned that rarest of honors for a cinematographer: his own section in your local alternative video store. *Idiot, you're looking in the wrong place!* Star 80 *is in the* Nykvist *section, not the Bob Fosse one!*

Sven Nykvist

Office Space. Mildly diverting 1999 comedy about cubi-cle life in corporate America, puzzlingly accorded classic status in Snob circles, where ritual mass viewings are common. The sole live-action feature by *Beavis and Butt-head* and *King of the Hill* creator Mike Judge, *Office Space* is representative of a whole strain of underperforming studio films that only Snobs "got," such as John Boorman's *Excalibur*, the Keanu-Swayze surf movie *Point Break*, the Val Kilmer vehicle *Real Genius*, and the PAULINE KAEL–anointed *Adventures of Buckaroo Banzai*.

Ophüls, Marcel. Keenly intelligent director of staggering, guilt-inducing documentaries that have variously indicted the French for collaboration with the Nazis, the Germans for their complacency during Hitler's reign, and the Americans for their involvement in Vietnam. Snobs who secretly haven't immersed themselves in his forbidding oeuvre are able to bluff their way through Ophüls bull sessions by dint of knowing about his Holocaust epic, *The Sorrow and the Pity* (1969), because of its status as a recurring gag in Woody Allen's *Annie Hall.* Especially knowing Snobs, on the other hand, can pronounce their familiarity with the work of Marcel's father, Max Ophüls, the director of such elegant, Kubrick-inspiring films as *La Ronde.*

Peckinpah, Sam. Ultramacho writer-director (1925–84) with a predilection for high body counts, balletic slo-mo violence, and ketchup-shortage-causing amounts of bloodletting. Fresno-born and educated at military schools (he served in the Marine Corps from 1943–47), Peckinpah eased into movies as a protégé of DON

SIEGEL's and made a name for himself with the Westerns *Ride the High Country* (1962) and *The Wild Bunch* (1969). Always abrasive and contrary, Peckinpah morphed in his later years into a Mexiphile counterculture stoner, albeit one with a distinctly unmellow view of man's primal savagery. His Snob-ratified classic, *Straw Dogs* (1971), about a wimpy, bespectacled American mathematician (Dustin Hoffman) who takes gruesome, uncharacteristic revenge on the ruffian oiks who rape his wife and besiege his house in a pastoral English town (and thereby becomes a "real man"), forever tagged Peckinpah an unreconstructed misogynist in feminist circles. Snobs also celebrate Peckinpah's alterna-Western *Pat Garrett and Billy the Kid* (1973), which, aside from having Bob Dylan and Kris Kristofferson in it, was mutilated by MGM, thus setting the stage for a post-

humous, Snob-titillating "as Sam would have wanted it" rerelease. Bizarrely, Peckinpah's last directing assignments were of two Julian Lennon videos, "Valotte" and "Too Late for Goodbyes," during the Beatle son's brief commercial heyday.

Sam Peckinpah

Polglase, Van Nest. Temperamental art director for RKO Pictures (1898–1968) in that studio's glory days, renowned for the sumptuous production designs of films as varied as *The Three Musketeers* (1935), *Gunga Din* (1939), and *Citizen Kane* (1941). Polglase gets his biggest Snob accolades, though, for the "Big White

Sets" he helped devise for such Fred Astaire and Ginger Rogers movies as *Top Hat* (1935) and *Shall We Dance?* (1937), highly stylized Art Deco expanses that afforded Fred and Ginger the opportunity to twirl into infinity. *Check out those Bakelite floors shined to a fare-thee-well; that's just* Polglase *at his most awesome.*

Platt, Polly. Polymathic, German-born set designer, screenwriter, producer, and actress, who, as the first Mrs. PETER BOGDANOVICH, is upheld by Snobs as the steadying influence behind the director's superior early work—it was she, for example, who acted on Sal Mineo's tip that Larry McMurtry's novel *The Last Picture Show* might make a good movie. Though she was only married to Bogdanovich from 1966 to 1970, Platt continued to work with him through 1973's *Paper Moon*, after which he lost the plot. Gracious even as her ex rampaged through a series of tootsies, Platt soldiered on respectably, writing Louis Malle's *Pretty Baby* (1978) and producing Wes Anderson's directorial debut, *Bottle Rocket* (1996).

Powell, Michael, and Emeric Pressburger. British-Hungarian filmmaking team beatified by the likes of Martin Scorsese and Francis Ford Coppola for their inventive if sometimes precious movies. Though most Snob-celebrated for *Black Narcissus, The Red Shoes,* and other expressionistic fantasias that their British production company, The Archers, turned out from 1942 to 1956, Powell (1905–90) and Pressburger (1902–88) started out making genre thrillers (among them *The Spy* *in Black, Contraband,* and *49th Parallel*) that are actually much more fun for normal moviegoers. After their amicable split in 1956, Powell went on to direct the uncharacteristic camp-horror movie *Peeping Tom* (1960), about a psycho-loner filmmaker who gores young lovelies to death with a sharpened prong of his tripod and films them dying. Though the film destroyed Powell's career, it *did* thrust the phrase "the male gaze" into the film-studies lexicon.

Raimi, Sam. Detroit-born director who, like fellow affable nerd-visionary PETER JACKSON, parlayed a series of wildly inventive low-budget splatter pics (chiefly, his *Evil Dead* movies of the 1980s) into an A-list career (the *Spider-Man* blockbusters). A friend and sometime collaborator of the Coen brothers' (he cowrote their film *The Hudsucker Proxy*), Raimi shares the brothers' acute sense of MOVIENESS—referencing forties pictures with frequent shots of big clocks, for example, and directing in coat and tie in homage to Alfred Hitchcock.

Ray, Nicholas. Romantically self-destructive director and Elia Kazan protégé (1911–79), exalted by auteurists for imprinting conventional Hollywood tales of fugitives and malcontents with his kinky, apocalyptic stamp; as every Snob knows, Jean-Luc Godard declared in 1958, "The cinema is Nicholas Ray." While best known for *Rebel Without a Cause* (1955), Ray wins his greatest Snob plaudits for *In a Lonely Place* (1950; Humphrey Bogart as a short-fused screenwriter),

Johnny Guitar (1954; Joan Crawford as an outcast saloon-keeper), and *Bigger Than Life* (1956; James Mason as a drug-addled schoolteacher). Ruined by drugs and booze, Ray was reduced to shooting soft-core porn in the seventies before semi-redeeming himself by collaborating with Wim Wenders on *Lightning Over Water* (1980), a documentary of Ray's own dying of cancer.

Ritz Brothers, the. Semi-forgotten trio of pointy-schnozzed vaudevillians-turned-film-zanies-of-the-thirties—Al, Jim, and Harry, born in Newark and raised in Brooklyn—championed by Comedy Snobs as tragically underrated geniuses forever in the shadow of the Marx Brothers, despite a scant filmmography whose best moments are the Fox comedy *The Three Musketeers* (1939) and some welcome comic interludes in whitebread Alice Faye musicals. PAULINE KAEL was a huge fan, as is Mel Brooks, who proclaimed the Ritzes funnier than the Marxes and put the aged Harry in *Silent Movie* (1976).

The Ritz Brothers

Road show. Old-fashioned screening technique from the days before nationwide openings, in which anticipation for a prestigious new film was built up by screening it in just a select few cities, with reserved seating and a higher-than-normal admission price. Often used in verb form by codgers dishing on their Hollywood adventures of yore. *We thought we had a hit, but it bombed when we* road-showed *it, so Jack Warner ordered us to shoot a schmaltzy new ending.*

Roeg, Nicolas. Pervy Brit director who established himself in the 1960s as an exacting cinematographer before forever cementing his reputation in both Film and Rock Snob circles with his 1970 directorial debut, *Performance* (codirected with the painter Donald Cammell), a curdled Swinging London bad-trip movie starring Mick Jagger, James Fox, naked ladies, and buckets of blood. Roeg followed through with three of the most unsettling films of the 1970s, *Walkabout, Don't Look Now,* and *The Man Who Fell to Earth.* His 1980 film *Bad Timing: A Sensual Obsession* marked the first of his repeated exploitations of his comely American wife, Theresa Russell, who would star (and strip) in seven of his films, most excruciatingly in *Bad Timing,* in which Art Garfunkel (!!!) has sex with her character's lifeless, comatose body.

Rohmer, Eric. Senior member of the FRENCH NEW WAVE directors (born in 1920), more sanctified by Snobs than his brethren for his insusceptibility to trends and his devotion to making talky films set in the "now," with his contemporary, middle-class Frenchies forever yakking about their sexual peccadilloes. Demonstrating his own Film Snobbery at an early age by changing his name from Jean-Marie Maurice Scherer in homage to Erich von Stroheim, Rohmer rose to become editor-in-chief of *CAHIERS DU CINÉMA,* moving on to directing features only in 1959, relatively late in comparison to his younger New Wave peers. Subsequently, he has conceived his films as cycles: the "moral tales" of the 1960s and '70s

(*My Night at Maud's, Claire's Knee*), the "comedies and proverbs" of the 1970s and '80s (*Pauline at the Beach, Full Moon in Paris*), and the "tales of the four seasons" of the 1990s (*A Winter's Tale, A Summer's Tale*, etc.). In 2004, Rohmer scandalized the Snob faithful by making his first genre picture, *Triple Agent*, an all-talk 1930s spy story without a single moment of action in it.

Rosenbaum, Jonathan. Industrious but mirthless film critic for the *Chicago Reader*; one of the few important film writers of the post-KAEL era. Given to chiding fellow Snobs about their ignorance of the IRANIAN NEW WAVE.

Rota, Nino. Italian movie composer closely associated with Federico Fellini and considered by Soundtrack Snobs to be in the league of ENNIO MORRICONE and LALO SCHIFRIN, his profile lower only because he has been dead since 1979. Most of Fellini's major works (*8½, La Dolce Vita*) are infused with Rota's trademark combination of fairground queasiness and nostalgic flourishes. Having also worked with Francis Ford Coppola (*The Godfather*) and Luchino Visconti (*The Leopard*), Rota is the Snob's preferred choice for evoking CINECITTÀ languor and decadence.

Nino Rota

Russell, Ken. Extravagant, overstuffed, campy director of extravagant, overstuffed, campy films, many of which are music-oriented (*The Music Lovers, Lisztomania*), many of which are lurid, sex-steeped bad acid trips (*The Devils, The Lair of the White Worm*), and some of which are both (*Tommy*, based on the Who's rock opera). First attracting Snob attention in 1969 with an overheated adaptation of D. H. Lawrence's *Women in Love* (featuring the exposed penises of Alan Bates and Oliver Reed), Russell went on to score an unlikely mainstream hit with *Altered States* (1980) before effectively doing in his career with *Whore* (1991), a NICOLAS ROEG–like exercise in Theresa Russell (no relation) abuse was meant as a riposte to cheerful prostitute pictures like *Pretty Woman*.

Sarris, Andrew. Brooklyn-born film critic and theorist best known for popularizing the AUTEUR THEORY, and for arousing the ire of PAULINE KAEL with his totemic 1968 book *The American Cinema: Directors and Directions 1929–1968*, in which he categorized directors by preference, prompting Kael to deride him, to his face, as a "list queen." His gentlemanly, hypeless prose has remained consistent since 1960, when he began writing for the *Village Voice*. Married to the fellow film-critster Molly Haskell, Sarris now plies his trade for the *New York Observer* and as a trainee Snob–adored lecturer at Columbia University.

Schifrin, Lalo. Modish Argentinean film scorer, second only to ENNIO MORRICONE on the modern-cool index. Known for his urgent, suspense-stoking compositions of the 1960s and '70s (for *Bullitt, Dirty Harry*,

Enter the Dragon, and the TV show *Mannix*, among other commissions), Schifrin found his status among postmodernist Snobs further enhanced when MTV-spawned director Brett Ratner asked him to score 1998's surprise hit *Rush Hour*.

Lalo Schifrin

Schneider, Bert. Acerbic counterculturist producer who, by virtue of his crankiness and withdrawal from the film business in the early 1980s, is the least-known major figure of the *EASY RIDERS, RAGING BULLS* generation of American film mavericks—which has only piqued Snob interest in him further. While a vice president at the Screen Gems division of Columbia Pictures in the mid-sixties, he started up the *Monkees* TV series with fellow iconoclasts Bob Rafelson and Jack Nicholson (the bespectacled talking dummy in the prefab group's beach pad was named "Mr. Schneider" in his honor), before moving on to produce, among other movies, *Easy Rider, Five Easy Pieces, The Last Picture Show*, and *Days of Heaven*. In a rare public appearance, Schneider, accepting the 1975 Academy Award for best documentary for the anti–Vietnam War film *Hearts and Minds*, made a proto–Michael Mooreish speech in which he read aloud a cable from an ambassador from the Provisional Revolutionary Government of Vietnam, so upsetting Oscars host Bob Hope that Hope had Frank Sinatra take the stage to read a disclaimer stating that Schneider's views were his own, not those of the Academy or the schmoozy Hollywood elite.

TEN
"LOST
MASTERPIECES"

There is no greater rallying cry for Film Snobs than the "lost masterpiece," the cinematic work of art done in by public indifference, reckless cutting by unvisionary bean-counters, or its author's own eccentricities and/or travails. Herewith, some of the most Snob-celebrated specimens of the genre.

Purported masterpiece: *Greed*, 1925, directed by Erich von Stroheim

"Lost" because: The ever-extravagant von Stroheim presented MGM production head Irving Thalberg with a *nine-hour* initial cut of his adaptation of Frank Norris's novel *McTeague*, about a burly miner-turned-dentist whose life falls apart after his wife wins $5,000 in the lottery; Thalberg balked at the movie's interminable length, ordering it cut down, and finally snatched control of it from von Stroheim, whittling it down to 140 minutes and tossing out the unused footage (though a 1999 salvage job by Turner Classic Movies, using production stills instead of moving-picture images, runs four hours).

Purported masterpiece: *Queen Kelly*, 1928, directed by Erich von Stroheim

"Lost" because: This time, von Stroheim intended to work outside the studio system, getting financing from Joseph Kennedy, then Gloria Swanson's lover, to make what he planned to be a five-hour epic about a convent girl, played by Swanson, who falls for a prince and is then exiled to a brothel in East Africa; Kennedy pulled the plug when he realized how outré von Stroheim's vision was, and only in the 1980s did a "restored" version appear, cobbled together with rediscovered footage, outtakes, and stills.

Purported masterpiece: *The Magnificent Ambersons*, 1942, directed by Orson Welles

"Lost" because: The workaholic Welles left for Brazil to work on a new picture almost immediately after filming wrapped on this adaptation of Booth Tarkington's elegaic novel, naïvely assuming that he would have no trouble editing the film via long-distance correspondence; while he was gone, RKO Pictures, fearing a flop, hacked the two-hours-plus film Welles envisioned down to 88 minutes and patched on an incongruous, workmanlike new ending, trashing the cut Welles footage and all prints of his long rough cut, thereby ensuring the picture's commercial doom and cementing Welles's status forevermore as a fat Hollywood pariah.

Purported masterpiece: *Ace in the Hole*, 1951, directed by Billy Wilder

"Lost" because: Riding high after *Sunset Boulevard*, Wilder unleashed a jaw-droppingly cynical film about a ferocious, washed-up newspaper reporter (Kirk Douglas) who ruthlessly exploits the predicament of a man trapped in a cave-in. Way too caustic for audiences of the time, the film was quickly retitled *The Big Carnival* by Paramount, but to no avail, and the shamed studio withdrew it from circulation, enabling its mystique to grow among Snobs, who lament that the film remains unavailable on DVD.

Purported masterpiece: *Fear and Desire*, 1953, directed by Stanley Kubrick

"Lost" because: Kubrick was so embarrassed by this, his first feature—an expressionistic war allegory, made for $9,000, starring a twenty-year-old Paul Mazurksy—that after its initial release he managed to prevent it from being screened again commercially for forty years; in 1994, after the George Eastman House in Rochester restored a print, New York's Film Forum showed the film for a week despite Kubrick's protests, and it hasn't been seen anywhere since.

Purported masterpiece: *Don Quixote*, 1950s and '60s, directed by Orson Welles

"Lost" because: Welles, scorned by the studios after the *Ambersons* experience, spent the rest of his life scaring up independent financing for his, er, quixotic effort to adapt the Cervantes novel to film, shooting in fits and starts, without a script, in Mexico and Europe, but died in 1985, leaving behind several hours' worth of edited and unedited footage, much of which remains scattered in cinematheques and private collections around the world. In 1992, the Spanish filmmaker Jess Franco, who had been a second-unit director on Welles's *Chimes at Midnight*, assembled his own cut of the film, but Snobs dismiss it as an abomination.

Purported masterpiece: *Kaleidoscope*, mid-1960s, directed by Alfred Hitchcock

"Lost" because: MCA-Universal, the studio with whom Hitchcock was working, didn't like his idea of making a radical, French New Wave–influenced, verité-style film told from the point of view of an attractive young man who happens to be a gay rapist and serial killer (with nude scenes to boot); what remains is approximately an hour of the experimental, soundless footage that Hitchcock managed to film, bits of which are occasionally screened to salivating Snob audiences.

Purported masterpiece: *Superstar: The Karen Carpenter Story*, 1987, directed by Todd Haynes

"Lost" because: Haynes didn't clear the rights to the Carpenters' music, and Richard Carpenter was not amused by Haynes's actually rather poignant 43-minute Carpenters biopic enacted entirely by Mattel Barbie and Ken dolls, complete with Karen Carpenter's anorexia death; Richard prevented the film's release, though it has circulated widely among Snobs as a bootleg.

Purported masterpiece: *The Local Stigmatic*, 1989, directed by Al Pacino and David F. Wheeler

"Lost" because: Pacino has never released the film, based on a one-act 1960s play by an Englishman named Heathcote Williams, in which he and Paul Guilfoyle star as Cockney hotheads who engage in cryptic conversation and deliver a savage beating to a famous actor they meet in a bar—though, very occasionally, Pacino allows the film, which he has never edited to his satisfaction, to be screened at museums, and DVD plans are afoot.

Purported masterpiece: *The Beaver Trilogy,* 2000, directed by Trent Harris

"Lost" because: Music-rights clearance issues have prevented the release of this bizarre, affecting trio of half-hour short films, all of which concern a talent-show performance of Olivia Newton-John's song "Please Don't Keep Me Waiting." The first performance was fortuitously caught on video by Harris in 1979, when he filmed a real-life amateur from Beaver, Utah, who called himself Groovin' Gary. Harris then filmed an unknown Sean Penn reenacting Gary's performance in 1981, and *then* filmed an unknown Crispin Glover reenacting Gary's performance in 1984. The trilogy was only ever screened on the festival circuit in 2000–2001, and Snobs contend that Penn appropriated Gary's laugh for his portrayal of Jeff Spicoli in *Fast Times at Ridgemont High.*

Schoonmaker, Thelma. Martin Scorsese's devoted editor, renowned for shaping crafted, finished films out of the miles of footage the hyperkinetic director shoots. Having met Scorsese while both were film students at New York University, she edited his first feature (*Who's That Knocking at My Door*, 1968) and every movie of his since *Raging Bull* (1980). In 1984, Schoonmaker compounded her Snob-pantheon status by marrying the aged MICHAEL POWELL.

Schrader, Paul. Whiz screenwriter and occasional director beloved by Snobs for his facility with brutal, sordid subject matter. Raised in a severe Calvinist household in Michigan—he never even saw a film until he was eighteen years old—Schrader first emerged in the early seventies as a heavy-duty film critic and PAULINE KAEL protégé before selling his screenplay for *The Yakuza* (1975), a story about an American (Robert Mitchum) who gets mixed up with the Japanese mob. Since, he has written Martin Scorsese's two most inflammatory films (*Taxi Driver, The Last Temptation of Christ*) and directed a sequence of fraught, atmospheric dramas redolent of crime, scuzz, and sexual perversion, including *Hardcore, American Gigolo, The Comfort of Strangers*, and *Auto Focus*—as well as the uncharacteristic Michael J. Fox mullet-musical *Light of Day*. His little-seen 1985 film, *Mishima*, about the great Japanese novelist who committed suicide, is a Snob cause célèbre.

Paul Schrader

Second-unit director. A deputy to a film's main director whose job is to shoot scenes and footage that don't require the presence and immediate supervision of the main director, often action sequences and expositional location shots. Many a second-unit director, having overseen his own semiautonomous production crew, has eventually graduated to supremo-director status, though Snobs glory in knowing the names of such career second-unit specialists as Yakima Canutt (who was also an ace stuntman in John Wayne movies) and B. Reeves Eason. *No disrespect to Paul Verhoeven, but the real reason* RoboCop *rocks is that Monte Hellman was the uncredited* second-unit director.

Sevigny, Chloë. *Jolie-laide* New York ingenue and fashion plate whose deadpan features have been put to opportunistic use by independent directors filming MEDITATIONS ON ennui, youthful disaffection, and just-plain callow stupidity. An immediate indie sensation as an HIV-infected teenager in Larry Clark's *Kids* (1995), Sevigny has been the favored masochist-martyr-pinup of art-house directors ever since, up to and including her infamous subjugation–to–Vincent Gallo scene in *The Brown Bunny* (2003).

Shaw Brothers. Hong Kong–based studio and distribution company named for its Shanghai-born founders, brothers Runme and Run Run Shaw, who cut their teeth in the movie business in Singapore in the 1920s and '30s, making low-budget pictures for Malay audiences. By the late fifties, their small production company had morphed into the estimable Shaw Brothers Ltd., which had its own huge backlot and cranked out hundreds of martial-arts pix and other genre films over the next two decades, effectively inventing the idea of Hong Kong cinema. Though the studio more or less ceased production in the mid-1980s (Runme died in '85), the Shaw name continues to elicit awe and respect among Martial Arts Snobs, not to mention astronomers and crowned heads; Run Run had an asteroid belt named after him in the sixties, and was knighted by Queen Elizabeth in 1984.

ShoWest. Trade convention put on in Las Vegas every March by the National Association of Theater Owners; renowned for being the first place that the major studios show trailers for their upcoming features, and, therefore, for being much less of an endurance test than SUNDANCE. *Dude, the new John Woo got tons of buzz at* ShoWest; *we're so there on opening day.*

Siegel, Don. American-born, Cambridge-educated director and Clint Eastwood mentor (1912–91) who earned Snob plaudits by virtue of having directed the prison drama *Riot in Cell Block 11*, the original *Invasion of the Body Snatchers*, and the Eastwood masterworks *Dirty Harry* and *Escape from Alcatraz*. Like SAMUEL FULLER, Siegel elicits strong public endorsements from wannabe-toughster Snobs trying to make up for dermatological and penile shortcomings; unlike Fuller, Siegel was more bemused than flattered by the auteur treatment he received in France.

Sight & Sound. Unexpectedly accessible-to-civilians Film Snob magazine, noted for listing the full cast and crew of each film it reviews; published monthly by the British Film Institute. Piques the momentary interest of non-Snobs every ten years when it conducts its favorite-films poll of more than two hundred critics and directors, which *Citizen Kane* inevitably wins (as it has since 1962).

Sirk, Douglas. Prime purveyor of the lavish and lachrymose "women's pictures" of the 1950s. A refugee from Hitler's Germany, Sirk transformed himself into America's premier soapster, elevating the schlock melodramas *Magnificent Obsession, Written on the Wind,* and *Imitation of Life* into Snob classics with his keen eye and prescient kitsch sensibility (as evidenced by Dorothy Malone's suggestive fondling of a model oil derrick in *Written on the Wind*). Snob auteur Todd Haynes paid painstaking homage to Sirk with 2002's *Far from Heaven.*

Douglas Sirk

Southern, Terry. Satirical novelist (*Candy, The Magic Christian*) and counterculture hero (included in the pantheon on the cover of *Sgt. Pepper's Lonely Hearts Club Band*) whose foray into screenwriting in the 1960s produced some of that decade's most subversive films— *Dr. Strangelove* (1964), *Barbarella* (1967), and *Easy Rider* (1969). The seventies were less kind, however, with Southern surfacing only to make token appearances in NICOLAS ROEG's *The Man Who Fell to Earth* and the Rolling Stones documentary *COCK-SUCKER BLUES* (in which his druggy state suggested a possible cause for his downturn in production), and, by 1980, he was reduced, not unlike fellow underground godhead NICHOLAS RAY, to working on a porn flick, *Electric Lady*. Nevertheless, he remained surrounded by groovy friends (ex-Beatles, Pythons, and his spiritual heir, Michael O'Donoghue of *Saturday Night Live*) in his later years, and, at his death in 1995, left behind a stack of unfilmed screenplays that, Snobs assert, could yield a gem of a film for Spike Jonze or Alexander Payne.

Spader, James. Blond, leanly handsome actor who, after a spate of college-boy roles in the 1980s, sidestepped the usual grab for leading-man status, and, instead, to the delight of an adoring Snob constituency, pursued a career as a character actor specializing in amoral white-collar creeps in such films as DAVID CRONENBERG's *Crash* (1996) and Steven Shainberg's *Secretary* (2002). In so doing (and in taking a similar role in TV's *Boston Legal*), Spader has attained the status of A-list wacko, alongside DEN-NIS HOPPER, John Malkovich, and Christopher Walken, without the nuisance of being a wizened survivor or funny-looking mannerist.

James Spader

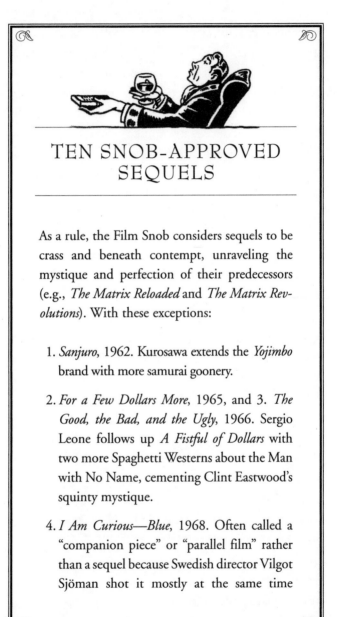

TEN SNOB-APPROVED SEQUELS

As a rule, the Film Snob considers sequels to be crass and beneath contempt, unraveling the mystique and perfection of their predecessors (e.g., *The Matrix Reloaded* and *The Matrix Revolutions*). With these exceptions:

1. *Sanjuro*, 1962. Kurosawa extends the *Yojimbo* brand with more samurai goonery.

2. *For a Few Dollars More*, 1965, and 3. *The Good, the Bad, and the Ugly*, 1966. Sergio Leone follows up *A Fistful of Dollars* with two more Spaghetti Westerns about the Man with No Name, cementing Clint Eastwood's squinty mystique.

4. *I Am Curious—Blue*, 1968. Often called a "companion piece" or "parallel film" rather than a sequel because Swedish director Vilgot Sjöman shot it mostly at the same time

as *I Am Curious—Yellow*, essentially delivering an alternate version of his soft-core "voyage of sexual discovery."

5. *Stolen Kisses*, 1968. Actually more of an entrant in a series (the five Antoine Doinel movies) than a sequel, but Truffaut hits his stride three films into the cycle begun with *The 400 Blows*, even surpassing that film in official Snob estimation.

6. *The Godfather, Part II*, 1974. But the less said about *Part III*, the better.

7. *French Connection II*, 1975. Zero-inspiration title, but surprisingly inspiring direction by John Frankenheimer, who takes over the Popeye Doyle franchise from Billy Friedkin.

8. *The Road Warrior*, 1981. More fun than *Mad Max*. But the less said about the mullet-fest follow-up, *Beyond Thunderdome*, the better.

9. *Silent Night, Deadly Night 3: Better Watch Out!*, 1989. Not even good for a C-grade slasher pic, but held dear by Snobs because its cult director, Monte Hellman (*Two-Lane Blacktop*), hasn't made a movie since.

10. *Toy Story 2*, 1999. The film that made Snobs grudgingly take Pixar seriously.

Spaghetti Westerns. European shoot-'em-up genre that blossomed in the early 1960s, just as John Ford–style American Westerns were on the wane, and flourished into the mid-seventies. So named because they were financed mostly by Italian production companies (though shot mostly in Spain), Spaghetti Westerns were grimmer, sillier, and far more violent and morally murky than their American counterparts, with ANTI-HERO leads in place of John Wayne hunks of granite. Though the lay viewer is most familiar with Spaghetti Western auteur Sergio Leone and his Clint Eastwood–starring Man With No Name trilogy—*A Fistful of Dollars, For a Few Dollars More,* and *The Good, the Bad, and the Ugly*—Spaghetti Snobs contend that the true genius of the genre was the unsung Sergio Corbucci, whose *Django* (1966; Franco Nero as the titular gunslinger) and *The Great Silence* (1968; mute, stubbly Jean-Louis Trintignant faces off with vile bounty hunter Klaus Kinski) mark the pinnacle of Spaghetti achievement.

-sploitation. *Alt.*-xploitation. Useful suffix that imputes a sense of scuzziness to whatever topic word it is attached to, resulting in an alluringly disreputable subgenre. Derived from the word *blaxsploitation,* which itself combined the words *black* and *exploitation* to describe the early-seventies boom of black-character films that featured rampant drug-dealing, crime-fighting, nudity, and outrageous 'fros. *I rate* Babette's Feast *ahead of* Tampopo *in the food-*sploitation *stakes.*

Steele, Barbara. Wild-eyed, witchie-poo B-movie actress equally at home playing seminude seductresses and scarifying goth girls in horror movies of the 1960s and '70s. English-born, Steele first made a splash playing two roles in the 1960 Italian horror film *Black Sunday* (no relation to John Frankenheimer's 1977 blimp-disaster movie) before being tapped by ROGER CORMAN to appear in one of his Edgar Allan Poe movies, *The Pit and the Pendulum* (1961), opposite Vincent Price. Steele matured into respectability as a TV producer, winning an Emmy for helping bring Herman Wouk's *War and Remembrance* to the small screen.

Barbara Steele

Sundance Film Festival. Annual January indie-film extravaganza held in Park City, Utah, scorned by Snobs as having long ago "sold out" to Big Hollywood—whose executives and actors, along with their media and PR parasites, throng the normally unassuming Old West ski town in their fur-trimmed finery—but grudgingly acknowledged as still the foremost proving ground for emerging directorial talent. The fruit of a collaboration between two originally separate entities—the Utah Film Commission, which had put on a lackluster film festival in Salt Lake City since 1978, and the Sundance Institute, founded in 1981 by Robert Redford as a way to nurture American independent filmmakers and to make use of the land he'd purchased in 1969 with dreams of developing an artists' colony—the Sundance Festival assumed cultural might in 1989, when twenty-six-year-old Steven Soderbergh's *Sex, Lies, and Videotape* won raves and saw the majors suddenly grappling for the right to distribute micro-budget films (such as the later Sundance hits *El Mariachi* and *The Blair Witch Project*). The glitzification of Sundance has begat a variety of more-indie-than-thou alternative festivals, among them Slamdance, Digidance, Nodance, and, inevitably, TROMA ENTERTAINMENT's Tromadance.

Suzuki, Seijun. Japanese B-picture director of the 1960s whose violent CinemaScope action pictures grew increasingly eccentric as time went on, culminating in 1967's *Branded to Kill,* about a Yakuza hit man with a fetish for sniffing freshly steamed rice. Fired by his studio, Nikkatsu, for making "incomprehensible films" (a not entirely unfair charge), Suzuki spent years in the wilderness before being lionized by his burgeoning Snob constituency (which includes Quentin Tarantino and Jim Jarmusch). *Branded to Kill* has received the CRITERION COLLECTION treatment, and in 2001, Suzuki finally managed to shoot its sequel, whose title, *Pistol Opera,* aptly encapsulates the outlook of violence-loving Asian-cinema enthusiasts.

Tamiroff, Akim. Hirsute Russian character actor beloved for his swarthy, often comic turns in Orson Welles's films of the fifties (*Touch of Evil, Mr. Arkadin,* the unfinished *Don Quixote*) and seemingly every movie made in the 1940s. Valued by Snobs for the Welles connection and for being less known to lay film buffs than his contemporary Euro-eccentric Peter Lorre. *Orson always said to Cybill and me, "There's no one I liked working with better than* Akim Tamiroff."

Tarkovsky, Andrei. Russian director (1932–86) of stunning intellect and visual acuity, but afflicted with a glacial sense of pacing that makes watching his films not so much an entertainment choice as a lifestyle. His seven features, which include the original *Solaris* and the SVEN NYKVIST–shot *The Sacrifice*, are manna to Snobs for whom Jean Cocteau, Ingmar Bergman, and Alain Resnais are insufficiently opaque.

Tasty print. Grating Snob catchphrase for a museum-quality print of a restored film. *Film Forum had a* tasty print *of* The Manchurian Candidate—*the blacks were so deep!*

Third row, the. The only appropriate place for a true cinephile to sit, as per the dictum of the late Snob overlord and belle-lettrist Susan Sontag. Though the third row is said to provide the ideal perch from which to comfortably take in the MISE-EN-SCÈNE while unobstructed by fellow audience members, New York's Anthology Film Archives, in 1970, catered to the sociopathy of Film Snobs by opening its Invisible Cinema, in which partitions sectioned off every single seat, so the filmgoer saw nothing but the screen.

Todd-AO. Wide-screen process developed in the early 1950s by banty force-of-nature producer and Elizabeth Taylor–marryer Mike Todd, at a time when many studios and companies were developing such processes (others were Cinerama, CinemaScope, and Panavision) in response to the threat of TV. The ever-shrewd Taylor, for whom Todd was the only husband she didn't divorce (he died in a plane crash in 1958), demanded that 20th Century-Fox shoot *Cleopatra* (1963) in Todd-AO, since she, as Todd's heir, would stand to make more money off the film. Tech Snobs are favorably inclined toward Todd-AO, which fell out of favor in the early seventies, because its 70mm prints are made off of 65mm negatives (with the extra 5mm allotted to the soundtrack), producing a very high quality picture, whereas inferior widescreen processes are made off of 35mm negatives. *If you see* Airport, *you must see it in the original* Todd-AO *70mm, and not in the crappy 35mm anamorphic prints that most film societies have.*

Towne, Robert. Beardy, seen-it-all screenwriter and script-doctor extraordinaire of the *EASY RIDERS, RAGING BULLS* crowd, in contention with PAUL SCHRADER for the title of writer most entitled to auteur status. Yet another of ROGER CORMAN's protégés, Towne established himself as maverick Hollywood's secret weapon, doing uncredited polishes on *Bonnie and Clyde, The Godfather* (conjuring the garden scene between Michael and Don Corleone entirely from his imagination), and *Heaven Can Wait*, and writing (with full credit) the screenplays for *The Last Detail* (1973), *Chinatown* (1974), and *Shampoo* (1975)—an awesome trifecta that forever guaranteed him entrée into the Warren-and-Jack den of iniquity. Though his record as a director is spotty, with his Mariel Hemingway lesbo-athlete pageant *Personal Best* (1982) tanking and his Michelle Pfeiffer vehicle *Tequila Sunrise* (1988) doing respectable business, Towne, also a good buddy of Tom Cruise's and ROBERT EVANS's, is effectively bulletproof in Hollywood. *I remember riding with* Bob Towne *in the limo the night he won Best Screenplay for* Chinatown, *a celebratory cigar in my mouth and an awesome piece of ass in my lap.*

Robert Towne

Troma Entertainment. Gonzo independent production company in business since 1974, specializing in cheapo, cheerfully cheesy horror-comedies (*Class of Nuke 'Em High*, the *Toxic Avenger* series) and cheapo, cheerfully cheesy juggs-SPLOITATION movies (*Waitress! The First Turn-On!!*,), many of which are directed by Troma's irrepressible founder himself, Lloyd Kaufman. Kaufman, who has cultivated a bow-tied, ranting-libertine New York Jew persona—a sort of cleaned-up, slimmed-down, unbearded Al Goldstein with soft-core rather than hard-core proclivities—often takes to the road to teach a ROBERT McKEE–style seminar on filmmaking, based on his book *Make Your Own Damn Movie! Secrets of a Renegade Director.*

"AMERICA WAS NOT PREPARED!"

A Brief Guide to
Snob-Beloved "Way-Out" Movies

Between 1965 and 1970, Hollywood somehow countenanced the filming of several star-studded, nonsensical movies that were clearly made under the influence of drugs, or at least under the influence of panicky, post–*Dr. Strangelove* executives who wanted to reach out to people who were on drugs. This vogue for "way-out" or "freak-out" movies didn't last, given that these films invariably bombed and were heaped with critical scorn, but the Snob treasures this queasy period as a font of great, misunderstood cinema.

The Loved One, 1965
Trippy plotline: Englishman comes to Los Angeles to handle interment arrangements of uncle, discovers nasty subculture of hypercompetitive em-

balmers and funeral directors against grotesque
Hollywood backdrop; based on Evelyn Waugh
novella

Motley all-star cast: Milton Berle, James Coburn,
Liberace, John Gielgud, Tab Hunter, Robert
Morse, Jonathan Winters, Dana Andrews, Jamie
Farr, Bernie Kopell, Rod Steiger

Ironically deployed sports-world mascot(s): Los Angeles
Lakers announcer Chick Hearn

Snobworthy participant(s): Terry Southern (screenplay), Haskell Wexler (cinematography), Hal
Ashby (editing)

Lord Love a Duck, 1966

Trippy plotline: Nerdy, anarchist teen at progres-
sive California school, played by thirty-eight-
year-old Roddy McDowall, desperately woos
Tuesday Weld

Motley all-star cast: McDowall, Weld, Ruth Gordon,
Harvey Korman

Ironically deployed sports-world mascot(s): none

Snobworthy participant(s): George Axelrod, screenwriter of *The Manchurian Candidate* and *Breakfast at Tiffany's* (screenplay, direction)

Head, 1968

Trippy plotline: The Monkees get killed, but not
really, and embark on a series of sketches skew-

ering the plastic Establishment machine, with
interspersed Vietnam footage

Motley all-star cast: Monkees, Victor Mature,
Annette Funicello, Frank Zappa, Teri Garr, Toni
Basil

Ironically deployed sports-world mascot(s): Sonny
Liston, Ray Nitschke

Snobworthy participant(s): Bob Rafelson (screenplay, direction), Jack Nicholson (screenplay),
Bert Schneider (executive producer)

Skidoo, 1968

Trippy plotline: A retired gangster (Jackie Gleason)
unretires to make one last hit and embarks on
mad LSD trip while in prison

Motley all-star cast: Gleason, Carol Channing,
Groucho Marx, Mickey Rooney, Frankie Avalon,
Burgess Meredith, Frank Gorshin, Peter Lawford,
George Raft, Cesar Romero, Slim Pickens,
Roman Gabriel

Ironically deployed sports-world mascot(s): Roman
Gabriel

Snobworthy participant(s): Otto Preminger (direction), Harry Nilsson (music, including the
singing of every last film credit), Rudi Gernreich
(costumes)

Candy, 1968

Trippy plotline: Gorgeous college girl embarks on promiscuous journey of discovery of the meaning of life; based on Terry Southern's satirical novel of same name, itself based on Voltaire's *Candide*

Motley all-star cast: Richard Burton, Marlon Brando, Charles Aznavour, Ringo Starr, James Coburn, John Huston, Walter Matthau, Elsa Martinelli

Ironically deployed sports-world mascot(s): Sugar Ray Robinson

Snobworthy participant(s): Southern (novel, screenplay), Buck Henry (screenplay)

Myra Breckinridge, 1970

Trippy plotline: Voluptuous post-op transsexual moves from New York to L.A. and humiliates men, complete with a dildo rape; based on Gore Vidal's satirical novel of same name

Motley all-star cast: Raquel Welch, Rex Reed, Mae West, Farrah Fawcett, John Huston, Jim Backus, John Carradine, Tom Selleck

Ironically deployed sports-world mascot(s): none

Snobworthy participant(s): Reed (actor, pre-op "Myron" Breckinridge), Vidal (novel), Edith Head (West's costumes)

Tweed, Shannon. Former *Playboy* Playmate of the Year (1982) with an impressive, extensive, two-decade list of credits in B and C movies, most of them straight-to-video "erotic thrillers" that require her to be naked (such as *Night Eyes 2, Illicit Dreams,* and *Cannibal Women in the Avocado Jungle of Death*), but are, in the minds of hairsplitting Snobs, "exploitation films" rather than soft-core porn. Improbably patrician and un–San Fernando Valley–ish of appearance, Tweed has nevertheless borne the children of Kiss frontman Gene Simmons.

Two-reeler. A comic film short from Hollywood's Golden Age. (Most shorts ran about 20 minutes, or about two reels' worth of celluloid.) Though virtually all the great early film comics performed in two-reelers, the Snob generally uses the term to denote the low-humor slapstick shorts churned out in the 1930s and '40s by such acts as the Three Stooges and, even more cred-enhancingly, the forgotten two-reeler stalwarts Leon Errol and Edgar Kennedy. *Damon and Kinnear perform with the slapstick aplomb of an old* two-reeler *team.*

Un Chien Andalou. Landmark short from 1929, in which the surrealist tag team of artist Salvador Dalí and director Luis Buñuel pooled images from their dreams to form a halluci-natory nonnarrative 17-minute

Un Chien Andalou

film, the most indelible moment of which is a close-up of an eye being slashed, its aqueous humor spilling out. Though willfully irrational, the film, a perpetual campus favorite, is billed in the catalogue copy of FACETS VIDEO, as nearly all non-American films are, as a "jolting tale of desire."

Vidor, King. Sentimentalist American director of the 1920s–40s whose maudlin, often messagey films (especially the Depression-era homage to communal farming, *Our Daily Bread*) have been hailed by Snobs as masterpieces on account of their authentically audacious camera technique and technological innovation. Frequently confused by novice Snobs with the Hungarian-born director Charles Vidor (*Gilda*), who was no relation.

Weerasethakul, Apichatpong. Vanguard director of the burgeoning Thai cinema scene, admired by Snob trendspotters for his "beguiling" (i.e., incomprehensible) avant-garde films, and for the sheer frisson one gets from uttering his multisyllabic name (though he actually prefers to be called Joe). Weerasethakul's quasidocumentary *Mysterious Object at Noon* (2000) ends with the camera breaking while the sound clatters on as the crew tries to do repairs; *Blissfully Yours* (2002) has its opening credits 45 minutes into the film and features nonactors, improvised dialogue, and actual, explicit sex; and *Tropical Malady* (2004) begins as a love story between a country boy and a soldier and ends as a baffling allegory about a shape-shifting spirit.

Wexler, Haskell. Visually versatile cinematographer and auxiliary member of the *EASY RIDERS, RAGING BULLS* cool club, having shot, among other films, *Who's Afraid of Virginia Woolf?* (1966), *In the Heat of the Night* (1967), and *One Flew Over the Cuckoo's Nest* (1975), while helping out George Lucas on *American Graffiti* (1973) and TERRENCE MALICK and NÉSTOR ALMENDROS on *Days of Heaven* (1978). But Wexler's Snob calling card is his sole nondocumentary directorial effort, the woozy, of-its-time *Medium Cool* (1969), a MEDITATION ON media manipulation in which a TV-news cameraman (Robert Forster) gets caught up in the turbulence of the '68 Democratic National Convention in Chicago.

Whip pan. Jarring technique in which a handheld or tripod-mounted camera moves horizontally at high speed, resulting in a disorienting blur; used as both a transition technique (as in the old *Batman* TV series) and as a bravura kinetic flourish. *Those* whip pans *in* Raging Bull's *fight scenes are awesome, even if Scorsese ripped 'em off from Truffaut.*

Widmark, Richard. Snob-beloved noir and Western mainstay with fist-shaped face, renowned for his startling screen debut as hitman Tommy Udo in Henry Hathaway's *Kiss of Death* (1947), in which he cacklingly pushed a wheelchair-bound old lady down a flight of stairs to her death. Though a versatile, intelligent actor, he was prized in Hollywood for his ability to play psychos and heels in such movies as JOSEPH L. MANKIEWICZ's *No Way Out* (1950) and SAMUEL FULLER's *Pickup on South Street* (1953), in effect becoming the prototype for such upmarket villainy-specialists as DENNIS HOPPER, Gary Oldman, and John Malkovich.

WIP. Snob abbreviation for Women in Prison, the exploitation subgenre whose films reliably feature sadistic lesbian wardens, gratuitous shower scenes, and titillating-appalling catfights. Though the heyday of WIPs was the early 1970s, when ROGER CORMAN's New World Pictures released its Women's Penitentiary trilogy of *The Big Doll House, The Big Bird Cage,* and *Women in Cages* (all of which starred PAM GRIER), WIPs continue to be made by low-budget outfits to this day, and tastemaker directors such as John Waters and Quentin Tarantino have incorporated many stock WIP elements into their work.

Wire-fu. Modish Snob term for both the genre and the technique in which martial-arts actors are attached to wires and pulleys, the better to suggest such superhuman powers as the ability to leap great heights and to slowly pirouette through the air while dispatching of opponents with combination kicks. Pioneered by the action star Jet Li in Hong Kong movies in the 1980s, wire-fu reached the mainstream with *Crouching Tiger, Hidden*

Wire-fu

Dragon (2000) and the *Matrix* movies. Some martial-arts purists lament the growing popularity of wire-fu, preferring the "wireless," and therefore more audacious, stunts of vintage Jackie Chan. *Ching Siu-Tung's ninja extravaganza* Duel to the Death *is an awesome example of early* wire-fu.

Wiseman, Frederick. Tireless cinema verité documentarian who, since *Titicut Follies* (1967), an expose of ugly goings-on at a Massachusetts mental hospital, has regularly churned out trenchant, engrossing films that pique the otherwise undisturbed social consciences of Film Snobs. Telegraphing his earnestness with flat, unembellished film titles (*High School, Public Housing, Domestic Violence*), Wiseman makes few concessions to his viewers' scheduling needs or buttock comfort: *Near Death* (1989), about a Boston hospital's intensive care unit, runs six hours, while *Belfast, Maine* (1999), about a depressed fishing town, runs four.

Woronov, Mary. American B-movie actress whose Amazonian build and androgynous beauty posited her as a more elegant counterpart to BARBARA STEELE in the Snob-celebrated schlock movies of the 1960s, '70s, and '80s. While studying art at Cornell, Woronov fell into Andy Warhol's Factory scene, starring in his *The Chelsea Girls* (1966) before moving to Los Angeles and becoming the muse-costar of cuddly trash specialist and ROGER CORMAN protégé Paul Bartel, who cast her in such films as *Death Race 2000* (1975) and his crossover hit, *Eating Raoul* (1982). Like her square character in the latter film, Mary Bland, Woronov, though surrounded by lechers and freaks, is said to live a disappointingly straight life offscreen.

Zahn, Steve. Smallish, affable actor of regular-guy mien, exalted in Snob circles for his comedic performances in underperforming movies that only Snobs "got," such as *Safe Men* (1998), *Chain of Fools* (2000), and *Saving Silverman* (2001). Usually matched with a similarly game young actor in a "buddy" scenario. *Sam Rockwell was awesome in* Safe Men, *but I was really groovin' on the* Zahn!

Steve Zahn

Z Channel. Los Angeles–based pay-cable movie channel that began its life in 1974 as a sort of proto-HBO or Showtime, and then, upon its hiring of a febrile repertory-cinema Snob named Jerry Harvey as its programmer in 1980, became the obsession of film-savvy industry folk (Orson Welles and JOHN CASSAVETES were both fans in their dying days) and twitchy aspirants (such as the pre-success Quentin Tarantino and Alexander Payne). Broadcasting semi-forgotten oldies and newer films—such as a long version of Michael Cimino's fiasco Western *Heaven's Gate* with studio-excised footage reinstated—Harvey educated a generation of trainee Snobs and effectively invented the DIRECTOR'S CUT, only for the Z Channel to go under in 1989 as larger competitors and video rentals siphoned off its business. A despairing Harvey murdered his wife and killed himself in 1988, but his reputation has since been rehabilitated by a 2004 documentary lovingly compiled by Cassavetes's daughter Xan. *I first grooved to Nick Ray when I was squatting at a friend's place above the Strip and caught* In a Lonely Place *on the* Z Channel.

About the Authors

© Anne Day

DAVID KAMP is a longtime writer for *Vanity Fair*, where short versions of *The Film Snob*s Dictionary* and *The Rock Snob*s Dictionary* first appeared, and also contributes regularly to *GQ*. He lives in New York City.

© Antrim Caskey

LAWRENCE LEVI has written about films and film culture for *The New York Times, The Nation,* and many other publications, and was a colleague of Kamp's at *Spy*, the satirical monthly. He lives in Brooklyn.

About the Illustrator

ROSS MACDONALD's illustrations have appeared in many magazines, from *The New Yorker* and *Vanity Fair* to *Rolling Stone* and *The Wall Street Journal.* Two of his children's books, *Another Perfect Day* and *Achoo! Bang! Crash! The Noisy Alphabet*, have won *Publishers Weekly* Best Books of the Year for their categories. MacDonald lives in Connecticut with his wife, two children, four cats, two dogs, and a large collection of nineteenth-century type and printing equipment.